Emerging Patterns in Cybersecurity

Trends, Threats, and Strategies for a Resilient Digital Future

Siddharth Rajhans
Dr. Gaurav Kumar Arora

ARCCHIE
www.arcchieonline.com

Emerging Patterns in Cybersecurity

Trends, Threats, and Strategies for a Resilient Digital Future

Editor: Priyanka
Production Manager: Gaurav Mutreja
Cover design by Freepik and Vecteezy
Formatting & Indexing: Rahul

First Edition: June-2025
Reference: 2412217
Published by Arcchie Publications

ISBN-13 (paperback): 978-81-986981-1-7
ISBN-13 (ebook): 978-81-979768-6-5

Published by ARCCHIE PUBLICATIONS, Greater Noida, U.P. -201 306
and Printed at Repro India Ltd., Mumbai

www.arcchieonline.com

DISCLAIMER

The information contained in this book is for educational and informational purposes only. While the publisher and authors have made every effort to ensure the accuracy and completeness of the information provided, they assume no responsibility for any errors, omissions, or contrary interpretation of the subject matter contained herein. This publication is sold with the understanding that the publisher and authors are not engaged in rendering legal, accounting, or other professional services. If legal or expert assistance is required, the services of a competent professional should be sought. Any trademarks, service marks, product names, or named features are assumed to be the property of their respective owners and are used only for reference. There is no implied endorsement if we use one of these terms. The views and opinions expressed in this book are those of the authors and do not necessarily reflect the official policy or position of any agency, organization, employer, or company. The publisher does not warrant the performance, effectiveness, or applicability of any sites listed or linked to in the book.

JOIN US ON THE ARCCHIE PUBLICATIONS DISCORD SERVER

Connect with fellow readers, authors, and enthusiasts to discuss all things related to our publications and the exciting world of AI, programming, and learning. Share your insights, ask questions, and engage in vibrant discussions to expand your knowledge and inspire creativity. Take advantage of this opportunity to be part of a dynamic community dedicated to exploring the frontiers of technology and innovation. Join our Discord Server today and be part of the ARCCHIE Publications community!

https://discord.gg/z26SenmpEt

DEDICATED TO

To **Col. Inderjit Singh**, a great cybersecurity expert and my revered mentor. Your wisdom, guidance, and leadership have shaped my journey in ways that words cannot fully capture. **Inderjit** Sir – you remain forever in our hearts, and we strive to carry your legacy forward with pride and purpose.

- Dr. Gaurav Kumar Arora

FOREWORD

As more companies are dependent on software, apps, and their online services, their entire businesses are at risk. What if a hacker takes down your site? What if a virus ends your business? Companies like Microsoft, Amazon, Google, and Apple are going to do everything in their power to make sure that doesn't happen.

"Security is... our top priority – if we don't solve these security problems, then people will hold back."
– Bill Gates, founder of Microsoft

Bill Gates made a great point. If technology companies don't solve the security issues they encounter, then their businesses won't survive. Microsoft (plus Amazon, Google, and others) won't sell their software and services.

For the last few decades, I've worked as a technical writer and a program manager to make sure our websites and services were as secure as possible. That includes working on Microsoft Surface, Windows, Office, SQL Server, Power BI, Azure, Power Platform, and Copilot. That also extended to Google-on-Google Cloud. I've helped support engineering teams build security features and have written and led production on how-to and architectural content that has helped many engineers and architects build secure solutions. I've also written several books and whitepapers on these topics.
One thing I've learned is that you want to prevent the problem as much as possible. You want to approach security with passion, intensity, desperation, and even fear that you'd have as if your system was just compromised by a security breach and you were in jeopardy of losing your entire business.

"An ounce of prevention is worth a pound of cure."
-- Benjamin Franklin, USA Founding Father and Inventor

That's right! It's time for some classic Benjamin Franklin! What he meant was that it's far more valuable and easier to prevent the problem than it is for you to fix it. And this is very true in cybersecurity! Even if you spend a lot of time, money, and resources to secure your application or platform, it's far more important for you to invest in security than for you to deal with the outcomes of a successful attack on your software! If you wait to fix the problem after a security breach, then you're fixing a lot more than software! You also must rebuild your customers' faith in your product and service. You have to rebuild your reputation.

So, what part of the system needs to be secured?

"Hackers rarely know your full tech stack—and they don't need to."
— John McAfee, Cybersecurity Pioneer and Founder of McAfee

John McAfee is the founder of one of the most successful cybersecurity-focused companies in the world. He would know better than anyone that all you need is a single point of vulnerability in your platform, application, or system, and that's all it takes to ruin your day (and possibly your entire business). Even actions as simple as email breaches have led to countless people losing their jobs.

As you can imagine, cybersecurity tools and features are being created and improved every week to help combat this real problem. We've seen new components introduced to help secure infrastructure as a service (IaaS) cloud service, as well as new technologies and tools like AI-based security solutions.

In Emerging Patterns in Cybersecurity, Siddharth Rajhans and Dr. Gaurav Arora guide you through all the challenges you'll face when developing an application or cloud-based solution. The authors provide chapters that show you how to use AI and ML and blockchain solutions and how to secure quantum computing and cloud-based solutions. They provide you with knowledge about cybersecurity frameworks, governance, real-world case studies, and the future directions that cybersecurity will take you in.

Sit back, buckle up, and get ready to explore an immersive yet brisk tour of everything related to cybersecurity.

Ed Price
MBA in Technology Management,
Technical writer and program manager with 25+ years of experience in software
(including Microsoft, Google, IBM, and Nintendo)
Inventor/owner on three Microsoft patents
Author of 10 books, including technical books for adults (The Azure Cloud Native Architecture Mapbook and ASP.NET Core 5 for Beginners) and for kids (Meg the Mechanical Engineer and Learn to Program with Small Basic)

ACKNOWLEDGEMENT

This book is the result of the collective efforts, guidance, and support of many individuals and organisations who have contributed to our journey in the field of cybersecurity. We would first like to express our heartfelt gratitude to our families for their unwavering encouragement, understanding, and patience throughout the writing process. Their support has been the foundation that enabled us to pursue this endeavour with dedication and focus. We are deeply thankful to our mentors, colleagues, and students who have inspired us with their insightful discussions, challenging questions, and critical perspectives. Their inputs have enriched our understanding and shaped the contents of this book to ensure it remains relevant, practical, and impactful. Our sincere appreciation goes to the professionals and experts in the cybersecurity community whose research, innovations, and relentless commitment to protecting the digital world continue to set benchmarks for excellence and resilience. We are particularly grateful to industry leaders, research collaborators, and academic institutions who have provided us with platforms to learn, teach, and contribute to this evolving domain. We also extend our thanks to the editorial and publishing teams at Arcchie Publications for their meticulous guidance, professionalism, and commitment to maintaining the highest standards in bringing this book to life. Their efforts ensured that our vision was translated into a comprehensive and reader-friendly resource.

Finally, we dedicate this book to the global community of cybersecurity practitioners, students, and leaders who work tirelessly to safeguard our digital future. We hope that this book supports your learning, strengthens your strategies, and empowers you to build a safer, more resilient world.

-- Siddharth Rajhans, and Dr. Gaurav Kumar Arora

ABOUT THE AUTHORS

- **Siddharth Rajhans** is an international career diplomat, a world-renowned multilateral diplomacy, international relations, and public policy expert, a Harvard-educated technology educator and investor, a management thought leader & professor, and a distinguished TED speaker. In a career spanning across Singapore, India, and the US, Siddharth has worked with tech giants such as Apple, Inc. In April 2023, Siddharth was invited by Apple to inaugurate Apple's flagship retail store with CEO Tim Cook at Apple Saket, New Delhi. In addition to his current policy role at the UN, Siddharth is an avid academic, associated with Manipal University Jaipur as an Adjunct Professor and JECRC University Jaipur as a Chair Professor. He is on the board of Governors of an IB School, Prometheus in Noida, India.

- **Dr. Gaurav Kumar Arora** is a renowned cybersecurity expert, technology leader, and academic with over two decades of experience in the IT industry. He holds a PhD in Computer Science with a research focus on cybersecurity and emerging technologies. Throughout his career, Dr. Arora has worked extensively across diverse domains, including security architecture, cloud computing, and AI applications in security. Currently, he serves as a senior technology leader, driving strategic initiatives in cybersecurity for global organisations. He is also an active researcher and educator, mentoring students and professionals through academic programs and professional workshops. Dr. Arora has authored multiple books and research publications, contributing significantly to the knowledge base of the technology community. He is passionate about bridging the gap between academic research and practical industry solutions to address real-world cybersecurity challenges. Beyond his professional commitments, he actively participates in community initiatives promoting digital security awareness and ethical technology practices.
  Follow him on LinkedIn - https://www.linkedin.com/in/aroragaurav.

ABOUT THE TECHNICAL REVIEWER

Ritu Mittal has nearly 17 years of experience working with engineering software systems across various industries. Throughout her career, she has demonstrated versatility by taking on multiple roles and delivering a wide range of projects successfully. Currently, Ritu serves as a Project Manager in the security domain at IBM, where she leads a diverse global team of over 25 professionals. She is responsible for managing server-level security for more than 150 clients. Alongside her primary role, she actively guides and mentors several teams across different areas within the organization. Ritu is deeply committed to promoting diversity in the IT sector. As an active member of her company's Diversity & Inclusion initiative for Delhi NCR, she works to create an inclusive and supportive environment for all team members. She believes in leading, by example, a principle that has shaped her professional journey and continues to inspire those around her.

PREFACE

The world today is more connected than ever before. From the devices in our pockets to the critical infrastructures that power our cities, almost every aspect of modern life relies on complex digital systems. As this digital revolution continues to accelerate, so too does the scale, sophistication, and impact of cyber threats. We envisioned Emerging Patterns in Cybersecurity as a response to this rapidly evolving landscape. The idea for this book emerged from our collective experiences across academia, research, and industry, witnessing firsthand how cybersecurity has transformed from a niche technical concern into a global strategic priority. Cyber-attacks that once targeted isolated networks now threaten entire supply chains, critical infrastructures, and national security, affecting millions of lives in profound ways. Our goal with this book is critical yet straightforward: to empower professionals, students, technology leaders, and enthusiasts with knowledge about emerging threats and the strategies needed to mitigate them effectively. This is not merely a technical manual. Instead, it is a comprehensive guide that bridges foundational cybersecurity concepts with advanced topics like AI, blockchain, and quantum computing, all within the context of real-world applications and practical strategies. We have designed each chapter to build upon the previous one, starting with fundamental principles before diving into more complex and futuristic topics. Whether you are an experienced cybersecurity professional aiming to stay ahead of the curve, a student entering this dynamic field, or a business leader seeking to fortify your organisation's digital defences, this book offers actionable insights and strategic perspectives to help you make informed decisions. Importantly, we believe that cybersecurity is not just about technology, it is about people, processes, governance, and foresight. As threats continue to evolve, so must our approaches to security, resilience, and digital trust. Throughout this book, you will find real-world case studies, global standards and frameworks, and future-oriented discussions that prepare you to navigate an uncertain yet opportunity-rich cyber landscape. This book is a collaborative effort born out of our shared passion to educate, inspire, and prepare the next generation of cybersecurity leaders. We are deeply grateful to our peers, mentors, and the broader cybersecurity community whose work continues to drive innovation and resilience in this critical domain. As you embark on this journey through the pages ahead, we encourage you to think critically, challenge assumptions, and apply the learnings to make meaningful contributions in your professional endeavours. Cybersecurity is no longer optional; it is an essential pillar of our digital future.

We hope this book inspires you to become an agent of change, ensuring a secure and resilient digital world for generations to come.

What's Inside This Book

Chapter 1: Introduction to Cybersecurity – An overview of cybersecurity, its evolution, and its critical role in today's digital world.

Chapter 2: AI and Machine Learning in Cybersecurity – Exploring how AI and machine learning are transforming threat detection, response, and predictive security analytics.

Chapter 3: Blockchain and Cybersecurity – Understanding the role of blockchain in securing transactions, managing identities, and enhancing data integrity.

Chapter 4: Quantum Computing and Its Impact on Cybersecurity – Examining how quantum computing challenges traditional encryption and what it means for future security.

Chapter 5: Cloud Security Challenges and Solutions – A deep dive into securing cloud environments, compliance considerations, and best practices for cloud security.

Chapter 6: Cybersecurity Frameworks and Governance – Overview of global cybersecurity frameworks and strategies to build strong governance and security cultures.

Chapter 7: Real-World Case Studies – Lessons from notable cybersecurity incidents and success stories with practical applications.

Chapter 8: Future Directions in Cybersecurity – Exploring emerging technologies, predictive analytics, and how the threat landscape is expected to evolve.

Chapter 9: Conclusion and Actionable Strategies – Key takeaways and strategic steps to build resilient cybersecurity systems for the future.

For Whom This Book Is Intended

This book is ideal for:

- Cybersecurity professionals and analysts seeking insights into emerging threats and technologies.
- IT administrators and technology leaders are aiming to strengthen their organisation's security posture.
- Students and academics in cybersecurity and IT fields look for comprehensive and practical knowledge.
- Business leaders and decision-makers who need to understand cybersecurity risks and strategies for informed decisions.
- Technology enthusiasts are interested in the latest trends and advancements in digital security.

Errata

At **ARCCHIE Publications**, we are committed to delivering the highest-quality content in all our publications. We follow best practices to ensure the accuracy of our content to provide our readers with indulgent reading experience. We believe and understand that our readers are our best judges, and we always use their input and feedback from time to time to improve human errors, if any, that may occur during the publishing processes involved. We invite you to participate in our errata submission process to ensure our books remain accurate and up to date. Please help us reach out to readers who might have difficulties due to unforeseen errors. Please write to us at ***errata@arcchieonline.com***.

When submitting errata, please include the following information:
Book Title, Reference#, Author(s), Page Number, Description of the Error, Suggested Correction (if applicable)

The **ARCCHIE Publications** Family highly appreciates your support, suggestions, and feedback.

Sharing Your Perspective and Providing Feedback

Your perspective is invaluable to us, as it helps us enhance our content and gather your feedback. We warmly welcome all forms of feedback. Please feel free to send us an email at **feedback@arcchieonline.com**, mentioning the book title in the subject line of your message.

Book Review Invitation

We kindly invite you to share your thoughts. After you've read and engaged with this book, consider leaving a review on the platform where you acquired it. Your impartial feedback can greatly assist potential readers in making informed decisions. Your reviews provide valuable insights for us at **Arcchie**, helping us better understand your perspectives on our products, and they offer authors the chance to appreciate your feedback on their work.

Piracy

If you possess expertise in a particular subject and wish to participate in the creation or contribution to a book, please visit ***authors.arcchieonline.com***. We welcome you and assist you to start your authorship journey with **ARCCHIE PUBLICATIONS**.

TABLE OF CONTENTS

Chapter 1: Introduction to Cybersecurity 1

Understanding Cybersecurity 1

Evolution of Cyber Threats 2

Advanced Persistent Threats (APTs) 3

Summary 4

Chapter 2: AI and Machine Learning in Cybersecurity 5

Brief overview of cybersecurity challenges 5

Shortage of skilled cybersecurity professionals 8

The promise of AI/ML in addressing these challenges 10

Proactive Threat Hunting and Prediction 12

Benefits of Proactive Threat Hunting and Prediction 13

Improved security posture and incident response 13

Improving Incident Response Capabilities 14

Let us explore some AI/ML Fundamentals 15

Natural Language Processing (NLP) in Cybersecurity 19

Identifying Phishing Emails 20

Security Information and Event Management (SIEM) 28

Security Orchestration, Automation, and Response (SOAR) 29

Deep Learning Models: Autoencoders 33

Challenges and Considerations 38

Best Practices for Ethical AI/ML in Cybersecurity 43

The role of AI/ML in developing more resilient and secure systems 47

Conclusion 49

Chapter 3: Blockchain and Cybersecurity 50

Brief Overview of Blockchain Technology 30

Blockchain's Relevance to Cybersecurity ... 51
Blockchain's Role in Enhancing Cybersecurity ... 53
How DID Solves These Problems ... 57
Blockchain-Based Cybersecurity Solutions ... 60
Conclusion ... 72
Chapter 4: Quantum Computing and Its Impact on Cybersecurity ... 74
A Brief History of Quantum Computing ... 75
Basics of Quantum Computing ... 76
Why Quantum Computing Matters ... 77
Quantum Threats to Cryptography ... 79
Preparing for a Post-Quantum World ... 79
Opportunities Presented by Quantum Computing ... 81
Conclusion ... 82
Chapter 5: Cloud Security Challenges and Solutions ... 83
Introduction: The Cloud Security Landscape ... 83
Defining Cloud Computing ... 84
The Unique Security Challenges of the Cloud ... 85
Account Hijacking and Unauthorized Access: A Deeper Dive ... 90
Infrastructure Security in the Cloud ... 91
Emerging Threats in Cloud Security ... 95
Cloud Security Solutions ... 97
The Role of Emerging Technologies ... 110
Artificial Intelligence (AI) and Machine Learning (ML) in Cloud Security ... 112
Blockchain in Cloud Security ... 114
Future of Cloud Security ... 116
The Evolving Threat Landscape and Emerging Challenges ... 118
Conclusion ... 122

Chapter 6: Cybersecurity Frameworks and Governance 123

Global Cybersecurity Frameworks 123

NIST Cybersecurity Framework (CSF) 124

Risk Management Frameworks 134

Security Policies and Procedures 135

Compliance and Regulatory Adherence 136

Conclusion 139

Chapter 7: Real-World Case Studies 141

Preparing for the Quantum Computing Threat 142

Conclusion 143

Chapter 8: Future Directions in Cybersecurity 144

Predictive Analytics and Cybersecurity 144

Artificial Intelligence and Machine Learning in Threat Detection 145

Behavioral Analytics and Insider Threat Prevention 148

Future of Behavioral Analytics in Cybersecurity 154

Conclusion 161

Chapter 9: Conclusion and Actionable Strategies 162

Recap of Key Cybersecurity Trends 162

Steps Towards Building Resilience 163

Conclusion 164

1

Introduction to Cybersecurity

In today's digital world, cybersecurity has emerged as a critical discipline to protect individuals, organisations, and nations from malicious activities targeting their information systems. This chapter provides an overview of cybersecurity, its evolution, and its significance in the modern era. By understanding its foundations, readers can appreciate why robust cybersecurity strategies are vital for a resilient digital future. Cyber threats continue to evolve rapidly, posing significant challenges to individuals, businesses, and governments worldwide. This chapter examines the current threat landscape, discussing the types of attacks prevalent today, the methods by which threat actors operate, and the impact of these threats on cybersecurity practices.

In this chapter, we will discuss:

- Definition and scope of cybersecurity
- Evolution of cyber threats
- Importance of cybersecurity in the digital age
- Advanced persistent threats (APTs)
- Ransomware and malware evolution
- Social engineering attacks
- Impact of modern threats on systems and data

Understanding Cybersecurity

Cybersecurity refers to the practice of defending computers, servers, mobile devices, electronic systems, networks, and data from malicious attacks. It encompasses a wide range of practices, technologies, and processes designed to protect digital assets against unauthorised access, damage, or theft.

Cybersecurity involves

- **Network security:** Protecting internal networks from intruders by securing infrastructure and devices.

- **Application security:** Ensuring that software and applications are free from threats that could exploit vulnerabilities.
- **Information security:** Protecting data integrity and privacy both in storage and transit.
- **Operational security:** Managing and protecting data assets through defined processes and permissions.
- **Disaster recovery and business continuity:** Defining how organisations respond to cyber incidents to resume operations effectively.
- **End-user education:** Training users to recognise threats and use security best practices.

Evolution of Cyber Threats

Cyber threats have evolved significantly over the past decades. Initially, threats were mostly **viruses spread via floppy disks** or **basic network worms**. As technology advanced, attackers began exploiting internet connectivity, leading to the development of sophisticated **malware, ransomware, phishing attacks, and advanced persistent threats (APTs).**

Key milestones in cyber threat evolution include

- **1980s-1990s:** Emergence of computer viruses (e.g., Brain virus, Melissa macro virus).
- **2000s:** Rise of worms (e.g., ILOVEYOU, Code Red) and basic phishing attacks.
- **2010s:** Sophisticated ransomware (e.g., WannaCry) and state-sponsored attacks targeting infrastructure.
- **2020 onwards:** AI-powered attacks, deepfake-based social engineering, and threats leveraging IoT devices and cloud environments.

Attackers today leverage advanced tools, automation, and artificial intelligence to enhance their attack strategies, making proactive cybersecurity measures more crucial than ever.
Importance of Cybersecurity in the Digital Age.

The significance of cybersecurity has never been greater due to:

- **Explosion of data and connectivity:** With billions of interconnected devices, each endpoint becomes a potential vulnerability.
- **Digital transformation initiatives**, including cloud adoption, remote work, and SaaS solutions, expand organisational attack surfaces.
- **Critical infrastructure threats:** Power grids, healthcare systems, and financial institutions are prime targets, posing a significant risk to national security.
- **Financial and reputational damage:** Cyber breaches can result in substantial losses, regulatory fines, and irreparable damage to a brand's reputation.
- **Evolving compliance requirements:** Regulations like GDPR, HIPAA, and national data protection laws enforce stringent security and privacy mandates.

Cybersecurity is not just an IT concern, but a **strategic business imperative** that impacts every aspect of society.

Advanced Persistent Threats (APTs)

Advanced Persistent Threats (APTs) are targeted, sophisticated cyberattacks in which an unauthorized user gains access to a system and remains undetected for an extended period. Unlike typical attacks that aim for quick gains, APTs focus on long-term espionage or data theft.

Key characteristics of APTs include

- **Targeted nature:** Focused on specific organisations, often in government, defense, finance, or critical infrastructure sectors.
- **Stealth operations:** Attackers employ advanced techniques to maintain undetected access for extended periods.
- **Multiple attack vectors:** Utilising phishing, malware, and zero-day vulnerabilities to gain and maintain access.
- **Long-term objectives:** Gathering intelligence, intellectual property theft, or preparing for future attacks.

Example: The Stuxnet worm targeting Iran's nuclear facilities and the SolarWinds attack are notable examples of APTs conducted for espionage and sabotage.

Ransomware and Malware Evolution

Ransomware is one of the most significant threats today, where attackers encrypt an organisation's data and demand ransom payments for decryption keys.

Modern ransomware trends include:

- **Double extortion:** Attackers steal data before encryption, threatening to leak sensitive information if the ransom is not paid publicly.
- **Ransomware-as-a-Service (RaaS):** Cybercriminal groups sell ransomware tools to affiliates, making it accessible to non-technical attackers.
- **Targeting critical infrastructure:** Healthcare systems, pipelines, and municipal services have been targeted, leading to operational shutdowns.

Malware evolution

Traditional malware, such as viruses and trojans, has evolved into sophisticated strains that can evade antivirus tools through techniques like obfuscation, polymorphism, and fileless attacks. Malware is now often used as a payload in phishing or APT campaigns to maintain persistence and expand access.

Social Engineering Attacks

Social engineering exploits human psychology to gain unauthorised access to systems or data.

Common social engineering attacks include

- **Phishing:** Fraudulent emails impersonating legitimate organisations to steal credentials or deploy malware.
- **Spear phishing:** Targeted phishing attacks aimed at specific individuals, often executives or privileged users.
- **Vishing and smishing:** Voice phishing (also known as phone scams) and SMS phishing, targeting users with fake alerts or requests.
- **Business Email Compromise (BEC):** Impersonation of executives or vendors to redirect payments or extract sensitive data.

Impact: Social engineering remains highly effective due to human error and lack of awareness, making user training a critical cybersecurity defence strategy.

Impact of Modern Threats on Systems and Data

Modern cyber threats have a wide-ranging impact on organisations, including:

- **Operational disruptions:** Ransomware attacks can disrupt business operations, resulting in financial losses and reputational damage.
- **Data breaches:** Theft of customer, employee, or intellectual property data can result in regulatory fines and litigation.
- **Financial fraud:** Business email compromise and phishing can lead to unauthorised transactions and monetary losses.
- **Erosion of trust:** Continuous attacks erode user and customer trust in an organisation's security capabilities.

Summary

In this chapter, we learned:

- **Cybersecurity** refers to the protection of digital systems, networks, and data from malicious attacks.
- How **cyber threats evolved** from simple viruses to AI-powered, targeted attacks.
- **Cybersecurity is crucial today**, considering our dependence on digital systems for business continuity, safety, and national security.

In the next chapter, we will explore **"AI and Machine Learning in Cybersecurity"** to understand how emerging technologies enhance threat detection, response, and resilience strategies.

2

AI and Machine Learning in Cybersecurity

Over the past many years I have had the privilege of observing Silicon Valley companies from close quarters around work. This led to understand the best practices being incorporated in Cybersecurity by them and in the three chapters that I have authored in this book, I try and provide a comprehensive view around AI & Machine learning in Cybersecurity along with Blockchain and its implications in the Cyber security space.

I have also delved into Cloud security challenges and solutions - and interesting mix of use cases from Silicon Valley. The overall purpose of these chapters is to give you a holistic view of what the industry is doing around cybersecurity, how the academic community is helping build a dialogue around this and how researchers are further expanding this knowledge into actionable insights for the industry. Thus, my chapters are written meticulously over a three month period - backed by extensive work and research of over 15 years - from three distinct perspectives - Industry, academia and research. I hope you will love reading them and admire the depth of information you receive via this book.

Brief overview of cybersecurity challenges

Cybersecurity faces a constantly evolving set of challenges. Here's a brief overview:

- **The Rise of AI-Powered Attacks:** Artificial intelligence is increasingly being used by cybercriminals to automate attacks, making them more sophisticated and harder to detect. This includes AI-generated malware, deepfakes for social engineering, and autonomous botnets.
- **The Internet of Things (IoT) Explosion:** The growing number of interconnected devices creates a vast attack surface. Many IoT devices have weak security, making them vulnerable to exploitation and potential misuse in large-scale attacks.
- **Cloud Computing Vulnerabilities:** While cloud computing offers numerous benefits, it also introduces new security risks. These include data breaches, supply chain attacks,

and the complexity of securing data across multiple platforms.

- **The Human Factor:** Human error remains a significant cybersecurity challenge. This includes social engineering attacks like phishing, insider threats, and a lack of cybersecurity awareness among employees.
- **The Need for Constant Adaptation:** The cybersecurity landscape is constantly changing, requiring organizations to continuously adapt their defenses. This includes staying informed about emerging threats, investing in cybersecurity training, and implementing robust security measures.

These are just a few of the key cybersecurity challenges facing organizations today. Addressing these challenges requires a multi-layered approach that includes strong technology, robust security policies, and a well-trained and vigilant workforce. Increasing sophistication of cyber threats (ransomware, phishing, DDoS attacks). The cyber threat landscape is constantly evolving, with attackers becoming increasingly sophisticated in their methods.

This evolution is driven by several factors, including advancements in technology, the growing reliance on digital systems, and the increasing value of digital assets.

Ransomware

- **From simple encryption to multi-vector attacks:** Early ransomware attacks primarily focused on encrypting individual files on a victim's computer. However, modern ransomware attacks have evolved into multi-vector attacks that target entire networks, including servers, databases, and critical infrastructure.
- **Data exfiltration and double extortion:** Attackers are increasingly exfiltrating sensitive data before encrypting systems. This allows them to threaten to release the stolen data publicly if the ransom is not paid, adding another layer of pressure to victims.
- **Ransomware-as-a-Service (RaaS):** The rise of RaaS platforms has made it easier for cybercriminals with limited technical expertise to launch sophisticated ransomware attacks. These platforms provide attackers with the necessary tools and infrastructure, making ransomware attacks more accessible and widespread.

Phishing

- **From generic emails to highly targeted attacks:** Traditional phishing attacks relied on generic emails with obvious red flags. However, modern phishing attacks are highly targeted and personalized, making them more difficult to detect. Attackers use social engineering techniques to build trust with victims and trick them into clicking on malicious links or opening attachments.
- **Business Email Compromise (BEC):** BEC attacks target specific individuals within an organization, often executives or finance professionals. Attackers impersonate these individuals to trick employees into transferring funds or revealing sensitive

information.

- **Deepfakes and AI-powered impersonation:** The emergence of deepfakes and other AI-powered technologies is enabling attackers to create highly realistic audio and video recordings of individuals, making it even more difficult to detect and prevent social engineering attacks.

Distributed Denial of Service (DDoS) Attacks

- **From simple volumetric attacks to sophisticated multi-vector attacks:** Early DDoS attacks primarily focused on overwhelming a target's servers with traffic. However, modern DDoS attacks are more sophisticated and can target multiple layers of the network, including application layer protocols and infrastructure.
- **IoT botnets:** The proliferation of Internet of Things (IoT) devices has created a vast pool of vulnerable devices that can be easily compromised and used to launch large-scale DDoS attacks.
- **DDoS-for-hire services:** The availability of DDoS-for-hire services makes it easier for anyone to launch a powerful DDoS attack, regardless of their technical expertise.

Other Emerging Threats

- **Supply chain attacks:** Attackers are increasingly targeting software supply chains to compromise widely used software and applications. This allows them to infect a large number of victims with a single attack.
- **Cloud-based attacks:** The increasing reliance on cloud computing has created new attack surfaces for cybercriminals. Attackers are targeting cloud infrastructure and data to steal sensitive information or disrupt critical services.
- **Artificial intelligence (AI)-powered attacks:** AI is being used by both attackers and defenders in the cyber security landscape. Attackers are using AI to automate attacks, identify vulnerabilities, and evade detection. Defenders are using AI to detect and respond to threats more effectively.

AI-Powered Endpoint Detection and Response (EDR) Solutions

Another critical approach to proactive cybersecurity involves the use of **Endpoint Detection and Response (EDR) solutions** enhanced with AI.

For example, **CrowdStrike Falcon** is an advanced EDR platform that leverages artificial intelligence to provide comprehensive endpoint protection. It helps organizations to:

- **Stop breaches in real-time:** Uses AI and machine learning to identify and respond to both known and unknown threats quickly.
- **Protect endpoints comprehensively:** Continuously monitors and analyses endpoint activity to detect malicious behaviour and prevent attacks.

- **Prevent insider attacks:** Detects abnormal user behaviours indicative of insider threats, enabling swift mitigation.
- **Enhance productivity and resilience:** Automates threat detection and remediation, reducing manual workload for security teams and minimising operational disruptions.

By integrating AI into endpoint security, solutions like CrowdStrike empower organisations to **manage threats proactively**, strengthening their overall cybersecurity posture in today's evolving threat landscape.

- **Strong passwords and multi-factor authentication:** Using strong, unique passwords for all online accounts and enabling multi-factor authentication can help to prevent unauthorized access.
- **Regular software updates and security patches:** Keeping software up-to-date with the latest security patches can help to close known vulnerabilities.
- **Employee training and awareness:** Educating employees about the latest cyber threats and best practices for cybersecurity can help to prevent them from falling victim to attacks.
- **Advanced security technologies:** Implementing advanced security technologies, such as intrusion detection systems, firewalls, and endpoint security solutions, can help to detect and prevent cyberattacks.
- **Incident response planning:** Having a well-defined incident response plan in place can help to minimize the impact of a cyberattack and ensure a swift recovery.

By staying informed about the latest cyber threats and taking proactive steps to improve cybersecurity, individuals and organizations can better protect themselves from the growing dangers of the digital world.

Explosion of data and interconnected devices (IoT) The cyber threat landscape is constantly evolving, with attackers becoming increasingly sophisticated in their methods. This evolution is driven by several factors, including advancements in technology, the growing reliance on digital systems, and the increasing value of digital assets.

Shortage of skilled cybersecurity professionals

The global cybersecurity workforce faces a critical shortage, with the demand for skilled professionals far outpacing the supply. This gap poses significant risks to individuals, businesses, and governments alike, as the digital landscape becomes increasingly complex and cyber threats evolve rapidly.

Contributing Factors

- **Rapid Technological Advancements:** The ever-evolving threat landscape, driven by advancements in artificial intelligence, machine learning, and the Internet of Things

(IoT), requires a constantly evolving skillset.

- **Growing Cyberattacks:** The frequency and sophistication of cyberattacks, including ransomware, phishing, and DDoS attacks, are increasing dramatically, demanding a robust and skilled cybersecurity workforce to defend against them.
- **Lack of Skilled Professionals:** Despite the growing demand, the number of qualified cybersecurity professionals is not keeping pace.

This shortage is exacerbated by several factors:

  - **Limited educational programs:** Many educational institutions lack comprehensive cybersecurity programs to train and equip students with the necessary skills.
  - **Lack of awareness and interest:** Many students are unaware of the exciting and rewarding career opportunities available in cybersecurity.
  - **Competition from other sectors:** The technology industry, particularly in areas like artificial intelligence and data science, competes for talent with the cybersecurity field.

Consequences of the Shortage

- **Increased Vulnerability:** Organizations with inadequate cybersecurity defenses are more susceptible to cyberattacks, leading to data breaches, financial losses, reputational damage, and operational disruption.
- **Difficulty in Responding to Incidents:** A lack of skilled personnel can hinder an organization's ability to effectively respond to and recover from cyberattacks, prolonging the impact and increasing the potential for further damage.
- **Strained Resources:** Organizations are forced to spend significant resources on finding and retaining qualified cybersecurity talent, which can strain budgets and divert resources from other critical areas.

Addressing the shortage

- Investing in Cybersecurity Education:
  - Increase funding for cybersecurity education programs at all levels, from K-12 to higher education.
  - Develop industry-recognized certifications and professional development programs to enhance the skills of existing professionals.
  - Encourage greater collaboration between academia and industry to ensure that educational programs align with the evolving needs of the cybersecurity workforce.
- Promoting Cybersecurity as a Career Path:
  - Raise awareness among students and young professionals about the exciting and rewarding career opportunities available in cybersecurity.
  - Highlight the importance of cybersecurity in protecting critical infrastructure and national security.

    - Create mentorship programs to connect aspiring cybersecurity professionals with experienced practitioners.
- Leveraging Technology:
    - Utilize automation and artificial intelligence to augment the capabilities of existing cybersecurity teams.
- Develop innovative tools and technologies to improve threat detection, prevention, and response.
- Establishing Strong Process Guidelines and Reviews
    - Develop and implement robust cybersecurity process guidelines to standardize practices across the organisation.
    - Conduct **regular reviews and audits** of these processes to ensure they remain effective, up-to-date, and aligned with evolving threats and compliance requirements.
    - Foster a culture of continuous improvement, where processes are refined based on lessons learned from incidents, new technological developments, and regulatory changes.

The promise of AI/ML in addressing these challenges

Automation of threat detection and response: The automation of cybersecurity threat detection and response is a critical development in today's evolving threat landscape. As cyberattacks become increasingly sophisticated and frequent, relying solely on human intervention is no longer sufficient. Automation leverages technology to enhance security operations, improve efficiency, and accelerate response times.

Key Aspects of Automation in Cybersecurity

- Threat Detection
    - **Anomaly Detection:** Automated systems can continuously monitor network traffic, system logs, and user behavior to identify deviations from normal patterns. Machine learning algorithms can analyze vast datasets to detect subtle anomalies that may indicate malicious activity.
    - **Vulnerability Scanning and Assessment:** Automated tools can continuously scan systems and applications for vulnerabilities, such as outdated software, weak passwords, and misconfigurations. This allows for proactive remediation before exploitation.
    - **Endpoint Detection and Response (EDR):** EDR solutions leverage machine learning to analyze endpoint activity, detect malicious behavior, and respond automatically by isolating infected devices or blocking malicious processes.
    - **Security Information and Event Management (SIEM):** SIEM systems collect and analyze security logs from various sources, correlating events to identify

potential threats and provide real-time alerts.

- Threat Response
    - **Incident Response Orchestration and Automation (SOAR):** SOAR platforms automate repetitive tasks during incident response, such as threat intelligence gathering, containment actions, and communication with stakeholders.
    - **Automated Remediation:** Automated systems can automatically patch vulnerabilities, block malicious traffic, and isolate infected systems, minimizing the impact of an attack.
    - **Threat Hunting:** Automated tools can be used to proactively search for and investigate potential threats, such as hunting for malicious actors within the network.

Benefits of Automation

- **Improved Detection Speed and Accuracy:** Automated systems can analyze data much faster than humans, enabling quicker detection of threats and reducing the time to respond.
- **Enhanced Threat Visibility:** Automation provides a comprehensive view of the threat landscape by analyzing data from multiple sources and identifying hidden threats.
- **Reduced Mean Time to Respond (MTTR):** Automated response actions can significantly reduce the time it takes to contain and mitigate the impact of an attack.
- **Increased Efficiency and Productivity:** By automating routine tasks, security teams can focus on more strategic activities, such as threat hunting and incident investigation.
- **Cost Savings:** Automation can help to reduce the cost of security operations by minimizing the need for manual intervention and reducing the risk of costly data breaches.

Challenges and Considerations

- **False Positives:** Automated systems can sometimes generate false alarms, which can overwhelm security teams and waste valuable time.
- **Over-reliance on Automation:** While automation is crucial, it should not completely replace human oversight. Security professionals are still needed to interpret alerts, make critical decisions, and fine-tune automated systems.
- **Data Privacy and Security:** The collection and analysis of large datasets raise concerns about data privacy and security. Robust data protection measures must be implemented to ensure compliance with regulations.
- **Skill Gap:** A skilled workforce is needed to implement, manage, and maintain automated security systems.

The automation of cybersecurity threat detection and response is a critical step towards building a more resilient and effective security posture. By leveraging the power of technology, organizations can enhance their ability to detect and respond to threats quickly and efficiently, minimizing the impact of cyberattacks and protecting their valuable assets.

Proactive Threat Hunting and Prediction

Proactive Threat Hunting and Prediction: A Crucial Defense Against Evolving Cyber Threats In today's rapidly evolving threat landscape, traditional reactive security measures are often insufficient to protect organizations from sophisticated cyberattacks. Proactive threat hunting and prediction have emerged as critical components of a robust cybersecurity strategy. These proactive approaches shift the focus from simply reacting to incidents to proactively identifying and mitigating threats before they can cause significant damage.

Proactive Threat Hunting

Proactive threat hunting involves actively searching for and identifying threats that may have evaded traditional security controls. It's a deliberate and systematic process that goes beyond simply monitoring for alerts.

Threat hunters utilize a combination of techniques, including:

- **Hypothesis-driven analysis:** Developing and testing hypotheses about potential threats based on intelligence, threat intelligence feeds, and observed anomalies.
- **Advanced analytics and machine learning:** Employing sophisticated tools and techniques to analyze vast amounts of data, identify patterns, and detect subtle indicators of compromise (IoCs).
- **Deep dive investigations:** Conducting in-depth investigations of suspicious activity, following attack chains, and uncovering hidden threats.
- **Threat intelligence integration:** Leveraging threat intelligence feeds to gain insights into emerging threats and tailor hunting activities accordingly.

Proactive Threat Prediction

Proactive threat prediction aims to anticipate future threats by analyzing historical data, current trends, and emerging technologies. This involves:

- **Predictive modeling:** Utilizing machine learning algorithms to identify patterns and predict future attack vectors.
- **Vulnerability analysis and forecasting:** Identifying and prioritizing vulnerabilities in systems and applications, and predicting their potential exploitation.
- **Scenario planning:** Developing and simulating potential attack scenarios to assess their impact and identify potential mitigation strategies.
- **Staying informed about emerging threats:** Continuously monitoring the threat landscape, tracking new attack techniques, and adapting defenses accordingly.

Benefits of Proactive Threat Hunting and Prediction

- **Early detection of threats:** Proactive approaches enable organizations to identify and respond to threats before they can cause significant damage.
- **Reduced dwell time:** By detecting threats early, organizations can minimize the time attackers spend within their systems, reducing the potential impact of an attack.
- **Improved incident response:** Proactive threat hunting provides valuable insights into attacker tactics, techniques, and procedures (TTPs), which can improve incident response capabilities.
- **Enhanced security posture:** By proactively addressing vulnerabilities and anticipating threats, organizations can significantly strengthen their overall security posture.
- **Competitive advantage:** Organizations that proactively hunt for threats and predict future attacks gain a significant competitive advantage by minimizing disruption and maintaining business continuity.

Challenges and Considerations

- **Skill and expertise:** Effective threat hunting and prediction require highly skilled and experienced security professionals.
- **Resource requirements:** Implementing and maintaining proactive threat hunting programs can be resource-intensive, requiring significant investment in tools, technologies, and personnel.
- **False positives:** Advanced analytics and machine learning can sometimes generate false positives, which can waste valuable time and resources.
- **Keeping pace with the evolving threat landscape:** The threat landscape is constantly evolving, requiring continuous adaptation and refinement of threat hunting and prediction strategies.

Proactive threat hunting and prediction are essential components of a modern cybersecurity strategy. By proactively identifying and mitigating threats, organizations can significantly improve their resilience against cyberattacks, minimize business disruption, and protect their valuable assets in an increasingly complex and interconnected world.

Improved security posture and incident response

Improving Cybersecurity Posture and Incident Response: A Critical Imperative In today's hyper-connected world, robust cybersecurity is no longer a luxury; it's a necessity. Organizations of all sizes, from small businesses to multinational corporations, face a constant barrage of cyber threats, ranging from phishing attacks and malware infections to sophisticated ransomware and data breaches.

Strengthening Cybersecurity Posture

A strong cybersecurity posture involves a multifaceted approach that encompasses people, processes, and technology.

Key elements include

- Proactive Risk Assessment:
  - **Regular Vulnerability Assessments:** Conducting thorough and regular vulnerability assessments to identify and prioritize weaknesses in systems, applications, and networks.
  - **Threat Modeling:** Simulating potential attack scenarios to understand the potential impact and identify critical vulnerabilities.
  - **Risk Register Maintenance:** Maintaining an up-to-date risk register to track and prioritize identified risks, and document mitigation strategies.
- Robust Security Controls:
  - **Strong Authentication:** Implementing multi-factor authentication (MFA) for all user accounts to enhance access control.
  - **Data Encryption:** Encrypting sensitive data both in transit and at rest to protect it from unauthorized access.
  - **Network Security:** Implementing firewalls, intrusion detection/prevention systems (IDS/IPS), and other network security measures to monitor and control network traffic.
  - **Endpoint Security:** Deploying endpoint security solutions, such as antivirus, anti-malware, and endpoint detection and response (EDR) technologies, to protect devices from threats.
  - **Access Control:** Implementing least privilege principles to ensure that users have only the necessary access to perform their job functions.
- Security Awareness Training:
  - **Regular Training Sessions:** Conducting regular security awareness training programs to educate employees about common cyber threats, such as phishing, social engineering, and malware.
  - **Phishing Simulations:** Conducting phishing simulations to test employee awareness and identify areas for improvement.
  - **Promoting a Culture of Security:** Fostering a security-conscious culture within the organization where all employees are responsible for protecting company assets.

Improving Incident Response Capabilities

An effective incident response plan is crucial for minimizing the impact of a cyberattack.

Key elements include

- Incident Response Plan Development:

    - **Documented Procedures:** Developing and documenting clear and concise incident response procedures, including roles and responsibilities, communication protocols, and escalation paths.
    - **Regular Testing and Drills:** Regularly testing and rehearsing the incident response plan through tabletop exercises and simulations to identify and address any weaknesses.
- Rapid Detection and Containment:
    - **Real-time Monitoring:** Implementing real-time monitoring and threat intelligence feeds to detect and respond to threats quickly.
    - **Automated Response:** Utilizing automated tools and technologies to accelerate incident response actions, such as isolating infected systems and blocking malicious traffic.
- Post-Incident Review and Improvement:
    - **Conducting Thorough Reviews:** Conducting thorough post-incident reviews to analyze the incident, identify root causes, and implement corrective actions.
    - **Continuous Improvement:** Continuously improving the incident response plan based on lessons learned from past incidents.

Key Considerations

- **Budget Allocation:** Allocating sufficient budget for cybersecurity investments, including personnel, technology, and training.
- **Staying Informed:** Staying informed about the latest cyber threats and vulnerabilities through threat intelligence feeds and industry best practices.
- **Building Strong Partnerships:** Building strong partnerships with external security experts, such as managed security service providers (MSSPs), to enhance security capabilities.

By implementing these strategies, organizations can significantly improve their cybersecurity posture, minimize the impact of cyberattacks, and protect their valuable assets in today's increasingly complex threat landscape.

Let us explore some AI/ML Fundamentals

In this section we will explore, core part of AI/ML in Cybersecurity.

Machine Learning in Cybersecurity

Machine learning (ML) has become an indispensable tool in the fight against cyber threats. Its ability to analyze vast amounts of data, identify patterns, and make predictions empowers organizations to proactively defend against attacks and respond effectively to incidents.

Types of Machine Learning in Cybersecurity

1. Supervised Learning:

- **Definition:** In supervised learning, algorithms are trained on labeled data, meaning the desired output is known for each input. The algorithm learns to map inputs to the correct outputs by minimizing the difference between its predictions and the actual labels.

- Cybersecurity Applications:
    - **Intrusion Detection:** Identifying malicious network traffic by analyzing patterns in network data.
    - **Malware Classification:** Categorizing malware into families or types based on their behavior and characteristics.
    - **Phishing Detection:** Identifying fraudulent emails and websites designed to steal sensitive information.
    - **Spam Filtering:** Classifying emails as spam or legitimate.

2. Unsupervised Learning:

- **Definition:** Unsupervised learning deals with unlabeled data, allowing the algorithm to discover hidden patterns and structures within the data itself.
- Cybersecurity Applications:
    - **Anomaly Detection:** Identifying unusual or suspicious activities that deviate from normal behavior, such as unexpected login attempts or unusual network traffic patterns.
    - **User Behavior Analysis:** Identifying abnormal user behavior that could indicate a compromised account.
    - **Network Segmentation:** Grouping devices and users into logical segments based on their behavior and interactions.

3. Reinforcement Learning:

- **Definition:** Reinforcement learning involves training an agent to make decisions by interacting with an environment and receiving feedback in the form of rewards or penalties.
- Cybersecurity Applications:
    - **Security Policy Enforcement:** Developing and enforcing security policies that adapt to changing threats and user behavior.
    - **Automated Incident Response:** Automating the response to security incidents, such as isolating infected systems or blocking malicious traffic.
    - **Security Game Theory:** Modeling adversarial interactions between attackers and defenders to develop optimal defense strategies.

Benefits of Machine Learning in Cybersecurity

- **Proactive Threat Detection:** Machine learning algorithms can analyze large volumes of data to identify emerging threats and vulnerabilities before they can cause significant damage.
- **Improved Response Times:** Automated threat detection and response capabilities enable organizations to respond to incidents more quickly and effectively.
- **Reduced Costs:** By automating many of the tasks associated with cybersecurity, machine learning can help organizations reduce their overall cybersecurity costs.

- **Enhanced Security Posture:** Machine learning-based solutions can help organizations improve their overall security posture by identifying and mitigating risks more effectively.

Challenges and Considerations

- **Data Quality and Bias:** The accuracy and effectiveness of machine learning models depend heavily on the quality and representativeness of the training data. Biased data can lead to biased models that may make inaccurate predictions or discriminate against certain groups.
- **Explainability and Transparency:** Many machine learning models are complex and difficult to understand, making it challenging to explain how they arrived at a particular decision. This lack of transparency can make it difficult to trust and debug machine learning-based security systems.
- **Adversarial Attacks:** Attackers can attempt to manipulate or deceive machine learning models by feeding them malicious or misleading data.
- **Ethical Considerations:** The use of machine learning in cybersecurity raises ethical concerns, such as privacy, fairness, and accountability.

Machine learning is a powerful tool that can be used to enhance cybersecurity defenses and improve an organization's ability to detect, respond to, and mitigate cyber threats. However, it is important to be aware of the challenges and limitations of machine learning and to use it responsibly and ethically. By addressing these challenges and leveraging the power of machine learning, organizations can significantly improve their cybersecurity posture and protect themselves from the ever-evolving threat landscape.

Neural networks, convolutional neural networks (CNNs), recurrent neural networks (RNNs).

Deep Learning in Cybersecurity

Deep learning, a subfield of machine learning, utilizes artificial neural networks with multiple layers to extract complex features from data.

This capability makes it particularly effective in cybersecurity for tasks like:

- **Malware Detection:** Deep learning models, especially Convolutional Neural Networks (CNNs), can analyze the bytecode or executable files of malware to identify malicious patterns.
- **Intrusion Detection:** By analyzing network traffic, deep learning models can detect anomalies and identify malicious activities like DDoS attacks or data exfiltration.
- **Phishing Detection:** Deep learning models can analyze the content, sender, and links in emails to identify phishing attempts.

- **Vulnerability Assessment:** Deep learning can analyze code to identify potential vulnerabilities and security flaws.

Key Deep Learning Architectures in Cybersecurity

1. Neural Networks:

- **Foundation of Deep Learning:** Neural networks are interconnected nodes that mimic the human brain's structure. They learn by adjusting the weights of connections between nodes.
- **Cybersecurity Applications:** Basic neural networks can be used for simple classification tasks like spam filtering or basic malware detection.

2. Convolutional Neural Networks (CNNs):

- **Image and Pattern Recognition:** CNNs excel at analyzing data with grid-like structures, such as images or network traffic patterns.
- Cybersecurity Applications:
    - **Malware Analysis:** CNNs can analyze the visual representation of malware code or the network traffic generated by malware.
    - **Network Traffic Analysis:** CNNs can identify malicious traffic patterns by analyzing features like protocol usage, packet sizes, and source/destination addresses.
    - **Image-based Threat Detection:** CNNs can analyze images of suspicious documents or network diagrams to identify threats.

3. Recurrent Neural Networks (RNNs):

- **Sequential Data Analysis:** RNNs are designed to process sequential data, such as time series or text.
- Cybersecurity Applications:
    - **Intrusion Detection:** RNNs can analyze network traffic sequences to detect anomalies and identify attacks that evolve over time.
    - **Malware Analysis:** RNNs can analyze the sequence of system calls made by malware to identify malicious behavior.
    - **Threat Intelligence Analysis:** RNNs can analyze threat intelligence feeds to identify emerging threats and predict future attack trends.

Benefits of Deep Learning in Cybersecurity

- **Enhanced Accuracy:** Deep learning models can achieve high accuracy in detecting and classifying threats, even in complex and noisy environments.
- **Automation:** Deep learning can automate many cybersecurity tasks, such as threat detection and response, freeing up human analysts to focus on more strategic tasks.
- **Proactive Threat Hunting:** Deep learning models can proactively identify and respond to emerging threats, reducing the risk of successful attacks.
- **Adaptability:** Deep learning models can adapt to new and evolving threats by continuously learning from new data.

Challenges and Considerations

- **Data Requirements:** Deep learning models require large amounts of high-quality data for training, which can be challenging to obtain in the cybersecurity domain.
- **Explainability:** Deep learning models can be complex and difficult to understand, making it challenging to explain their decisions and debug errors.
- **Adversarial Attacks:** Attackers can attempt to manipulate or deceive deep learning models by feeding them malicious or misleading data.
- **Ethical Considerations:** The use of deep learning in cybersecurity raises ethical concerns, such as privacy, fairness, and accountability.

Deep learning is a powerful tool that can revolutionize cybersecurity by enabling more accurate, efficient, and proactive threat detection and response. By addressing the challenges and leveraging the power of deep learning, organizations can significantly improve their security posture and protect themselves from the ever-evolving threat landscape.

Natural Language Processing (NLP): For analyzing threat intelligence reports, identifying phishing emails

Natural Language Processing (NLP) in Cybersecurity

Natural Language Processing (NLP) is a field of artificial intelligence that focuses on enabling computers to understand, interpret, and generate human language. In the context of cybersecurity, NLP offers powerful tools for analyzing textual data, extracting valuable insights, and enhancing threat detection and response capabilities.

Analyzing Threat Intelligence Reports

Threat intelligence reports often contain valuable information about emerging threats, attack vectors, and adversary tactics. However, these reports are typically unstructured text, making it difficult for human analysts to quickly identify key insights and trends. NLP techniques can help automate the analysis of these reports by:

- **Extracting key information:** NLP can be used to extract key information from threat intelligence reports, such as:
    - **Indicators of Compromise (IOCs):** IP addresses, domain names, email addresses, and other indicators that can be used to identify and block malicious activity.
    - **Threat actor information:** Names, affiliations, and other details about the individuals or groups responsible for cyberattacks.
    - **Attack techniques and tactics:** Methods used by attackers to compromise systems, such as phishing, malware, and social engineering.
- **Identifying emerging threats:** By analyzing large volumes of threat intelligence data, NLP algorithms can identify emerging threats and patterns that may not be immediately apparent to human analysts.
- **Generating summaries:** NLP can be used to generate concise summaries of threat

intelligence reports, making it easier for security teams to quickly understand the key findings.

Identifying Phishing Emails

Phishing emails are a common cyber threat that can be used to steal sensitive information or install malware on victims' devices.

NLP techniques can be used to identify phishing emails by analyzing their content, including:

- **Identifying suspicious language:** NLP can be used to identify suspicious language patterns, such as:
    - **Urgency and fear-mongering:** Phishing emails often use urgent or threatening language to pressure victims into taking action.
    - **Impersonation:** Phishing emails may attempt to impersonate legitimate organizations or individuals.
    - **Suspicious links and attachments:** NLP can be used to identify suspicious links and attachments that may lead to malicious websites or downloads.
- **Analyzing sender information:** NLP can be used to analyze the sender's email address, domain name, and other information to identify potential red flags.
- **Detecting grammatical errors and typos:** Phishing emails often contain grammatical errors and typos, which can be a sign of a fraudulent message.

Benefits of NLP in Cybersecurity

- **Improved threat detection:** NLP can help security teams to more effectively detect and respond to cyber threats.
- **Increased efficiency:** NLP can automate many of the tasks associated with threat intelligence analysis, freeing up human analysts to focus on more strategic tasks.
- **Enhanced situational awareness:** NLP can provide security teams with a better understanding of the threat landscape and help them to make more informed decisions.

Challenges and Considerations

- **Data quality:** The accuracy of NLP-based cybersecurity solutions depends heavily on the quality of the data used to train the models.
- **Evolving threats:** Cyber threats are constantly evolving, which means that NLP models need to be continuously updated and retrained to remain effective.
- **Ethical considerations:** The use of NLP in cybersecurity raises ethical concerns, such as privacy and fairness.

Conclusion

NLP is a powerful tool that can be used to enhance cybersecurity defenses and improve an organization's ability to detect, respond to, and mitigate cyber threats. By leveraging the power of NLP, organizations can gain a better understanding of the threat landscape, improve their threat detection capabilities, and make more informed security decisions

- Now let's see AI/ML in Cybersecurity Applications:

AI/ML in cybersecurity empowers organizations to proactively defend against cyber threats. By analyzing vast datasets, AI/ML algorithms can:

- **Detect Anomalies:** Identify unusual network traffic, user behavior, or system activity that may indicate a cyberattack.
- **Classify Threats:** Categorize malware, phishing emails, and other threats with high accuracy.
- **Predict Future Attacks:** Analyze historical threat data to anticipate future attack vectors and vulnerabilities.
- **Automate Responses:** Trigger automated responses to security incidents, such as isolating infected systems or blocking malicious traffic.

These capabilities enable organizations to improve threat detection, accelerate incident response, and enhance their overall security posture.

- Threat Detection and Response:
    - **Intrusion Detection Systems (IDS):** Anomaly detection, signature-based detection, behavioral analysis

Intrusion Detection Systems (IDS)

Intrusion Detection Systems (IDS) are security tools designed to monitor network traffic and system activity for malicious activity or policy violations. They act as watchdogs, constantly analyzing data to identify potential threats and alert administrators.

Key Detection Methods:

1. Signature-Based Detection:
    - **Focus:** Identifies known threats by matching observed patterns to a database of known attack signatures (e.g., specific byte sequences in malware, common exploit patterns).
    - Strengths:
        - Effective against known threats.
        - Provides clear alerts with known attack details.
    - Weaknesses:
        - Limited to detecting known threats.
        - Ineffective against novel or zero-day attacks.
2. Anomaly-Based Detection:
    - **Focus:** Establishes a baseline of normal network behavior and flags any deviations from this baseline as potential intrusions.
    - Strengths:
        - Can detect unknown threats and zero-day attacks.
        - Proactive in identifying unusual activities.
    - Weaknesses:
        - Prone to false positives (flagging legitimate activity as malicious).

        - Requires careful configuration and tuning to minimize false alarms.
3. Behavioral Analysis:
    - **Focus:** Analyzes user behavior and system activity to identify deviations from expected patterns.
    - Strengths:
        - Can detect insider threats and unusual user activity.
        - Adapts to changing user behavior patterns.
    - Weaknesses:
        - Requires extensive data collection and analysis.
        - May require significant expertise to interpret results.

In Summary:

- IDS are essential tools for enhancing network security.
- Signature-based detection is effective against known threats, while anomaly-based detection can identify unknown attacks.
- Behavioral analysis focuses on user activity and system behavior to detect suspicious patterns.
- A combination of these methods often provides the most comprehensive protection.

Note:

- IDS are often deployed alongside Intrusion Prevention Systems (IPS), which can actively block or mitigate threats in real-time.
- Effective IDS implementation requires careful planning, configuration, and ongoing monitoring and maintenance

- **Malware Detection:** Static and dynamic analysis, sandboxing, file classification:

Malware Detection

Malware detection involves identifying and classifying malicious software to prevent harm to systems and data. Key techniques include:

- Static Analysis:
    - Examines malware without executing it.
    - Methods:
        - **Code analysis:** Analyzing the code for suspicious patterns, functions, and strings.
        - **File signature analysis:** Comparing file hashes to known malware signatures in databases.
        - **Metadata analysis:** Examining file headers, timestamps, and other metadata for anomalies.
    - **Advantages:** Fast, efficient, and doesn't require running the malware.
    - **Limitations:** May miss obfuscated or polymorphic malware.
- Dynamic Analysis:
    - Executes malware in a controlled environment (sandbox) to observe its

behavior.
  - Methods:
    - **Monitoring system calls:** Tracking interactions with the operating system (e.g., file system access, network connections).
    - **Analyzing network traffic:** Observing communication with external servers.
    - **Monitoring resource usage:** Tracking CPU, memory, and disk usage.
  - **Advantages:** Detects behavior-based malware and evasive techniques.
  - **Limitations:** Can be resource-intensive and may not detect all malicious behavior.
- Sandboxing:
  - Creates an isolated environment for executing suspicious files.
  - Protects the host system from potential harm.
  - Allows for safe observation of malware behavior.
- File Classification:
  - Categorizes files based on their type and purpose.
  - Helps identify suspicious files and prioritize analysis.
  - Techniques:
    - **Machine learning:** Using algorithms to classify files based on features like file size, file type, and content.
    - **Heuristic analysis:** Applying rules and patterns to classify files.

Key Considerations:
- **Evasion Techniques:** Malware can employ techniques to evade detection (e.g., polymorphism, obfuscation).
- **Zero-Day Threats:** Detecting new and unknown malware (zero-day threats) requires advanced techniques like anomaly detection and behavioral analysis.
- **False Positives/Negatives:** It's crucial to minimize false positives (flagging benign files as malicious) and false negatives (failing to detect malicious files).

By combining these techniques and staying updated on the latest threats, organizations can effectively detect and mitigate the risks posed by malware.

- **Phishing Detection:** Analyzing email content, sender reputation, URL analysis.

Phishing detection involves identifying and blocking emails designed to deceive recipients into revealing sensitive information or clicking on malicious links. Key techniques include:

1. Analyzing Email Content:
- **Suspicious Language:** Identifying urgent or threatening language, unusual greetings, grammatical errors, and requests for personal information.
- **Social Engineering Tactics:** Detecting attempts to manipulate emotions, create a sense of urgency, or exploit trust.

- **Impersonation:** Identifying emails that attempt to impersonate legitimate organizations or individuals.

2. Sender Reputation:
   - **Email Address Verification:** Checking the validity of the sender's email address and domain.
   - **Sender Authentication Protocols:** Utilizing techniques like SPF, DKIM, and DMARC to verify the authenticity of the sender.
   - **Blacklists and Whitelists:** Maintaining lists of known spammers and trusted senders.
3. URL Analysis:
   - **URL Structure:** Examining the URL for suspicious patterns, misspellings, or unexpected characters.
   - **URL Shorteners:** Avoiding clicking on shortened URLs (e.g., bit.ly, t.co) which can mask the true destination.
   - **Phishing URL Databases:** Comparing URLs to databases of known phishing websites.

Key Considerations:

- **Evolving Threats:** Phishing techniques are constantly evolving, requiring continuous adaptation of detection methods.
- **False Positives/Negatives:** Minimizing false positives (flagging legitimate emails as phishing) and false negatives (failing to detect phishing emails) is crucial.
- **User Education:** Training users to recognize phishing attempts is essential for effective defense.

By combining these techniques and staying informed about the latest phishing threats, organizations can significantly reduce their vulnerability to these attacks.

- Threat Hunting and Prediction:
  - **Vulnerability Assessment:** Identifying and prioritizing vulnerabilities.

Vulnerability assessment is a crucial cybersecurity process that involves identifying and prioritizing security weaknesses within an organization's systems, applications, and networks.

Key Aspects:

- Identification:
  - **Automated Scanning:** Employing tools to scan systems for known vulnerabilities (e.g., missing patches, outdated software, weak configurations).
  - **Manual Testing:** Conducting manual penetration tests to identify vulnerabilities that automated tools might miss.
  - **Vulnerability Databases:** Utilizing databases like the National Vulnerability Database (NVD) to stay informed about newly discovered vulnerabilities.
- Prioritization:
  - **Severity:** Assigning severity levels (e.g., critical, high, medium, low) based on factors like potential impact, exploitability, and ease of exploitation.

  - **Risk Assessment:** Considering the likelihood and potential impact of an attack exploiting the vulnerability.
  - **Business Impact:** Prioritizing vulnerabilities that pose the greatest risk to critical business functions and sensitive data.

Benefits:

- **Proactive Risk Mitigation:** By identifying and addressing vulnerabilities before they can be exploited, organizations can significantly reduce their risk of cyberattacks.
- **Improved Security Posture:** Regular vulnerability assessments help organizations maintain a strong security posture and comply with industry regulations.
- **Reduced Costs:** Addressing vulnerabilities proactively is often less expensive than dealing with the consequences of a data breach.
- **Enhanced Reputation:** Demonstrates a commitment to security and builds trust with customers and stakeholders.

Key Considerations:

- **False Positives/Negatives:** Minimizing false positives (flagging benign issues as vulnerabilities) and false negatives (missing critical vulnerabilities) is crucial.
- **Resource Allocation:** Prioritizing vulnerabilities effectively requires careful resource allocation to address the most critical issues first.
- **Continuous Monitoring:** Vulnerability assessments should be performed on an ongoing basis to keep pace with the evolving threat landscape.

By implementing a robust vulnerability assessment program, organizations can proactively identify and address security weaknesses, significantly reducing their risk of cyberattacks and improving their overall security posture.

Risk Assessment: Predicting potential attack vectors and their impact.

Cybersecurity Risk Assessment

A cybersecurity risk assessment is a systematic process used to identify, evaluate, and prioritize potential threats and vulnerabilities to an organization's IT systems and data. It helps organizations understand the potential impact of cyberattacks and make informed decisions about how to allocate resources to mitigate risks.

Key Steps in a Risk Assessment:

1. **Identify Assets:** Determine the organization's critical assets, including hardware, software, data, and intellectual property.
2. **Identify Threats:** Identify potential threats, such as malware, phishing, social engineering, and insider threats.
3. **Identify Vulnerabilities:** Identify weaknesses in the organization's security controls, such as outdated software, weak passwords, and misconfigurations.
4. **Analyze Risks:** Determine the likelihood and potential impact of each identified risk. This often involves considering factors such as the value of the asset, the severity of the

threat, and the effectiveness of existing controls.

5. **Prioritize Risks:** Prioritize risks based on their likelihood and potential impact. Focus on addressing the highest-priority risks first.
6. **Develop and Implement Mitigation Strategies:** Develop and implement appropriate security controls to mitigate identified risks. This may include implementing security technologies, improving security policies, and training employees on security best practices.
7. **Monitor and Review:** Continuously monitor the effectiveness of security controls and review the risk assessment on a regular basis to ensure that it remains accurate and relevant.

Benefits of Risk Assessment:

- **Improved Security Posture:** By identifying and addressing vulnerabilities, risk assessments help organizations improve their overall security posture and reduce their risk of cyberattacks.
- **Cost Savings:** Addressing risks proactively can save organizations significant costs associated with data breaches, legal fees, and reputational damage.
- **Better Decision-Making:** Risk assessments provide valuable insights that can inform strategic decision-making, enabling organizations to allocate resources effectively and prioritize security efforts.
- **Compliance:** In many industries, there is a legal or regulatory requirement to conduct risk assessments.

Key Considerations:

- **Involve Stakeholders:** Involve key stakeholders from across the organization, including IT, business units, and legal departments.
- **Use Appropriate Tools and Methodologies:** Utilize appropriate risk assessment tools and methodologies, such as threat modeling and vulnerability scanning.
- **Stay Informed:** Stay informed about the latest threats and vulnerabilities by monitoring industry news and threat intelligence feeds.

By conducting regular and thorough risk assessments, organizations can proactively identify and address cybersecurity threats, improve their security posture, and minimize the impact of potential cyberattacks.

Threat Intelligence Analysis: Correlating threat indicators and identifying emerging threats. Threat Intelligence Analysis. Threat intelligence analysis is the process of collecting, processing, analyzing, and disseminating information about cyber threats to inform decision-making and improve an organization's security posture.

Key Aspects:

- **Data Collection:** Gathering data from various sources, including:
    - **Internal sources:** Security logs, incident reports, vulnerability scans.

  - **External sources:** Threat intelligence feeds, open-source intelligence (OSINT), industry reports, government advisories.
- **Data Processing:** Cleaning, organizing, and structuring the collected data for analysis.
- Data Analysis:
  - **Correlating Threat Indicators:** Identifying relationships and patterns between different indicators of compromise (IOCs), such as IP addresses, domain names, and malware hashes.
  - **Threat Actor Profiling:** Analyzing the tactics, techniques, and procedures (TTPs) of threat actors to understand their motivations, capabilities, and targets.
  - **Identifying Emerging Threats:** Monitoring for new and emerging threats, such as zero-day vulnerabilities and novel attack techniques.
  - **Predictive Analysis:** Using machine learning and other techniques to predict future threats and attack scenarios.
- **Dissemination:** Sharing actionable intelligence with relevant stakeholders within the organization, including security teams, incident responders, and business leaders. Benefits of Threat Intelligence Analysis:
- **Proactive Threat Detection:** Enables organizations to proactively identify and mitigate threats before they can cause significant damage.
- **Improved Incident Response:** Provides valuable insights that can help organizations respond more effectively to security incidents.
- **Enhanced Security Posture:** Helps organizations to improve their overall security posture by identifying and addressing vulnerabilities and weaknesses.
- **Informed Decision-Making:** Provides the information needed to make informed decisions about security investments and resource allocation.

Challenges and Considerations:

- **Data Quality and Reliability:** Ensuring the accuracy and reliability of threat intelligence data is crucial.
- **Data Overload:** The volume of threat intelligence data can be overwhelming, making it difficult to identify and prioritize relevant information.
- **Skill Requirements:** Effective threat intelligence analysis requires specialized skills and expertise.
- **Evolving Threat Landscape:** The threat landscape is constantly evolving, requiring continuous monitoring and adaptation of threat intelligence strategies.

By effectively collecting, analyzing, and disseminating threat intelligence, organizations can gain a better understanding of the threats they face, improve their ability to detect and respond to attacks, and enhance their overall security posture

  - Let us now study "Security Operations":

Security Information and Event Management (SIEM): Correlation of security events, anomaly detection

Security Information and Event Management (SIEM)

SIEM is a cybersecurity solution that collects, analyzes, and correlates security-related data from various sources across an organization's IT infrastructure. This data includes logs from firewalls, servers, network devices, and other security systems.

Key Functions:

1. **Data Collection:** SIEM systems gather security event data from various sources, including:
    - **Network Devices:** Firewalls, routers, switches
    - **Servers:** Operating systems, databases, application servers
    - **Endpoints:** Workstations, laptops, mobile devices
    - **Security Appliances:** Intrusion Detection Systems (IDS), Intrusion Prevention Systems (IPS)
2. **Data Normalization and Correlation:** SIEM systems normalize data from different sources into a common format, making it easier to analyze. They then correlate events to identify patterns and relationships that may indicate a security threat. For example:
    - Multiple failed login attempts from the same IP address
    - Large data transfers outside normal business hours
    - Suspicious activity on a critical server
3. **Anomaly Detection:** SIEM systems utilize machine learning algorithms to identify unusual or suspicious activity that deviates from normal behavior. This includes:
    - **User Behavior Analysis:** Identifying unusual user activity, such as accessing sensitive data outside of normal working hours or logging in from an unexpected location.
    - **Network Traffic Analysis:** Detecting unusual network traffic patterns, such as high volumes of traffic to or from a specific IP address or unusual protocols.
4. **Alerting and Reporting:** SIEM systems generate alerts when suspicious activity is detected and provide real-time dashboards and reports to help security teams investigate and respond to incidents.

Benefits of SIEM:

- **Improved Threat Detection:** By correlating security events and identifying anomalies, SIEM systems can detect threats that might otherwise go unnoticed.
- **Faster Incident Response:** SIEM systems provide real-time visibility into security events, enabling organizations to respond quickly to threats.

- **Reduced Risk:** By proactively identifying and mitigating threats, SIEM systems can help organizations reduce their risk of cyberattacks.
- **Compliance:** SIEM systems can help organizations comply with regulatory requirements, such as PCI DSS and HIPAA.

Key Considerations:

- **Data Volume:** SIEM systems generate and process large volumes of data, requiring significant storage and processing capacity.
- **False Positives:** SIEM systems may generate false positives, requiring careful tuning and configuration to minimize false alarms.
- **Skill Requirements:** Effective use of SIEM requires skilled security analysts to interpret alerts and investigate incidents.

By effectively implementing and managing a SIEM solution, organizations can significantly improve their ability to detect, respond to, and mitigate cyber threats

Security Orchestration and Automation (SOAR): Automating security workflows, incident response playbooks.

Security Orchestration, Automation, and Response (SOAR)

SOAR is a cybersecurity technology that streamlines and enhances an organization's ability to detect, investigate, and respond to cyber threats. It combines three key elements:

- **Orchestration:** SOAR platforms connect and coordinate various security tools and technologies within an organization's infrastructure. This integration allows for seamless information sharing and coordinated responses.
- **Automation:** SOAR automates repetitive and time-consuming tasks, such as data collection, threat intelligence enrichment, and basic incident response actions. This frees up security analysts to focus on more strategic and complex issues.
- **Response:** SOAR provides a centralized platform for managing incident responses, including:
    - **Incident Triage:** Prioritizing and categorizing security alerts.
    - **Investigation:** Gathering and analyzing evidence related to security incidents.
    - **Containment:** Implementing containment measures to limit the impact of an attack.
    - **Remediation:** Taking corrective actions to address the root cause of the incident.
    - **Reporting:** Generating reports on security incidents for analysis and future planning.

Key Benefits of SOAR:

- **Increased Efficiency:** Automation streamlines processes, allowing security teams to respond to threats more quickly and efficiently.
- **Reduced Response Times:** Faster response times minimize the impact of cyberattacks and reduce the risk of data breaches.
- **Improved Accuracy:** Automation reduces the risk of human error, ensuring consistent and accurate responses to incidents.
- **Enhanced Visibility:** SOAR provides a centralized view of security events and incidents, improving visibility across the organization.
- **Cost Savings:** By automating tasks and improving efficiency, SOAR can help organizations reduce the cost of security operations.

Incident Response Playbooks

SOAR platforms utilize "playbooks" to guide and automate incident response processes. Playbooks are step-by-step instructions that outline the actions to be taken during a security incident. These playbooks can be customized to fit specific organizational needs and threat scenarios.

Key Considerations:

- **Integration:** Successful SOAR implementation requires careful integration with existing security tools and technologies.
- **Data Quality:** The quality of data fed into the SOAR platform is crucial for accurate analysis and effective response.
- **Skill Requirements:** While SOAR automates many tasks, skilled security analysts are still needed to oversee the process, interpret results, and make critical decisions.

By leveraging SOAR technology, organizations can significantly enhance their cybersecurity posture, improve their ability to respond to threats, and minimize the impact of cyberattacks.

AI/ML Techniques in Cybersecurity

AI/ML techniques are revolutionizing cybersecurity by enabling automated threat detection, rapid response, and proactive defense.[1] These technologies analyze vast datasets to identify anomalies, classify threats (like malware and phishing), predict future attacks, and automate responses.[2] For example, machine learning algorithms can analyze network traffic to identify suspicious patterns, classify malware based on their behavior, and predict the likelihood of a successful attack.[3] This empowers organizations to improve threat detection, accelerate incident response, and enhance their overall security posture

Anomaly Detection

Statistical methods: Outlier detection, clustering. Statistical methods play a crucial role in cybersecurity by providing powerful tools for analyzing data and identifying anomalies.

- **Outlier Detection:** This technique identifies data points that significantly deviate from the expected norm. In cybersecurity, outliers can indicate suspicious activity, such as:
  - **Unusual login attempts:** Logins from unexpected locations or at unusual times.
  - **Abnormal resource usage:** Unexpected spikes in CPU, memory, or network traffic.
  - **Deviations from normal user behavior:** Uncharacteristic file access patterns or software installations.
- **Clustering:** This technique groups similar data points together. In cybersecurity, clustering can be used to:
  - **Identify groups of compromised systems:** Grouping systems with similar malware infections or attack patterns.
  - **Detect botnets:** Grouping systems that are part of a botnet based on their communication patterns.
  - **Classify threats:** Grouping different types of malware or attacks based on their characteristics.

By applying these statistical methods, organizations can:

- **Improve threat detection:** Identify suspicious activity and potential threats more effectively.
- **Enhance incident response:** Gain a better understanding of the scope and impact of security incidents.
- **Improve security posture:** Identify and address vulnerabilities more proactively.

Example:
Imagine a network with a typical baseline of network traffic. Outlier detection could identify sudden spikes in traffic from a specific IP address, potentially indicating a Distributed Denial of Service (DDoS) attack. Clustering could group systems exhibiting similar unusual activity, suggesting a coordinated attack or a widespread malware infection.
Key Considerations:

- **Data Quality:** The accuracy of statistical methods depends heavily on the quality and completeness of the data.
- **False Positives/Negatives:** It's important to minimize false positives (flagging legitimate activity as malicious) and false negatives (failing to detect malicious activity).
- **Contextual Analysis:** Statistical analysis should be combined with other security measures and expert analysis to ensure accurate threat assessment.

By effectively utilizing statistical methods, organizations can significantly enhance their cybersecurity defenses and improve their ability to detect, respond to, and mitigate cyber threats.

Machine learning algorithms: Support Vector Machines (SVM), Isolation Forest

Both Support Vector Machines (SVM) and Isolation Forest have found important applications in cybersecurity, each with its strengths. Here's a breakdown:

1. Support Vector Machines (SVM)
   - **The Gist:** Imagine you have data points representing "normal" and "malicious" activity. SVMs try to find the clearest possible line (or hyperplane in higher dimensions) to separate these categories. They aim for the biggest "margin" between the groups, making the classification more robust.
   - In Cybersecurity:
     - **Malware Detection:** An SVM can be trained on features of files (size, code snippets, etc.) to classify them as malware or safe.
     - **Intrusion Detection:** Network traffic patterns can be fed to an SVM to distinguish between normal activity and intrusions like DDoS attacks.
     - **Phishing Detection:** SVMs can analyze email features (sender, content, links) to identify phishing attempts.
2. Isolation Forest
   - **The Gist:** This algorithm is excellent at finding outliers. It works by randomly partitioning data. The idea is that anomalies are "easier" to isolate – they'll get separated from the rest of the data with fewer partitions.
   - In Cybersecurity:
     - **Anomaly Detection:** Isolation Forest can flag unusual network traffic, login attempts, or system behavior that deviates significantly from the norm.
     - **Intrusion Detection:** It can detect suspicious connections or activities that stand out from typical network usage.
     - **Malware Detection:** Files with highly unusual characteristics or behavior can be identified as potential malware.

Why These Algorithms Are Useful:

- **Accuracy:** Both can be very accurate at identifying threats.
- **Efficiency:** SVMs can be fast, especially with optimizations. Isolation Forest is also relatively efficient for anomaly detection.
- **Versatility:** They can be used for many different cybersecurity tasks.

Things to Keep in Mind:

- **Data is Key:** Both need good quality data to learn effectively.
- **Outliers Matter:** SVMs can be a bit sensitive to outliers in the training data.
- **Interpretability:** Understanding *why* an SVM made a decision can sometimes be tricky.

In short: SVMs are great for finding clear boundaries between categories (like malware vs. safe files), while Isolation Forest excels at spotting the unusual "needles in the haystack" that might represent a threat.

Deep learning models: Autoencoders

Autoencoders are a type of neural network used in deep learning, and they have some interesting applications in cybersecurity. Here's a breakdown:

How Autoencoders Work:

An autoencoder has two main parts:

1. **Encoder:** This part takes input data (like network traffic data or file features) and compresses it into a lower-dimensional "latent space" representation. Think of it like creating a compressed summary of the data.
2. **Decoder:** This part takes the compressed representation and tries to reconstruct the original input data as accurately as possible.

The network is trained to minimize the difference between the original input and the reconstructed output. The idea is that the autoencoder learns to capture the essential features of the data in the compressed representation.

Why This Is Useful for Cybersecurity:

- **Anomaly Detection:** This is the most common application. Autoencoders learn what "normal" data looks like.When presented with anomalous data (like a malicious network connection or a suspicious file), the autoencoder will struggle to reconstruct it accurately. The difference between the input and the output (the "reconstruction error") will be high, flagging the data as potentially malicious.
    - *Example:* An autoencoder trained on normal network traffic will have a high reconstruction error when given data from a DDoS attack, as the attack traffic will deviate significantly from the normal patterns.
- **Feature Extraction:** The compressed representation learned by the encoder can be used as a set of features for other machine learning models. This can be useful for tasks like malware classification, where the autoencoder can extract relevant features from the raw file data.
- **Dimensionality Reduction:** Cybersecurity data can be very high-dimensional (lots of features). Autoencoders can reduce this dimensionality, making it easier to analyze the data and train other models.

Example Scenarios:

- **Intrusion Detection:** An autoencoder can be trained on normal network traffic. High reconstruction error on new traffic suggests an intrusion.
- **Malware Detection:** Autoencoders can analyze file characteristics. A file that's hard to

reconstruct might be malware.

- **Botnet Detection:** Botnet traffic often has specific patterns. Autoencoders can be used to detect deviations from normal traffic, which might indicate botnet activity.

Advantages:

- **Unsupervised Learning:** Autoencoders can be trained on unlabeled data, which is often readily available in cybersecurity.
- **Anomaly Detection:** They are excellent at finding unusual data points.

Challenges:

- **Training Data:** They still need a good amount of "normal" data to train effectively.
- **Complexity:** Designing and tuning autoencoders can be complex.
- **Explainability:** Understanding *why* an autoencoder flagged something as anomalous can be difficult.

Autoencoders offer a powerful approach to anomaly detection and feature extraction in cybersecurity, especially in situations where labeled data is scarce.
They are a valuable tool in the fight against evolving cyber threats.

Classification

Supervised learning: Naive Bayes, decision trees, random forests

Supervised learning algorithms are incredibly useful in cybersecurity because they can learn from labeled data to make predictions about new, unseen data. Here's a breakdown of three popular ones:

1. Naive Bayes

- **The Idea:** This algorithm is based on Bayes' theorem and assumes that the features used for classification are independent of each other (the "naive" assumption). It's surprisingly effective despite this simplification.
- In Cybersecurity:
    - **Spam/Phishing Detection:** Analyzing email content to classify emails as spam/phishing or legitimate.
    - **Malware Classification:** Classifying files as malicious or benign based on features like file type, size, and code snippets.

2. Decision Trees

- **The Idea:** Decision trees create a tree-like structure to make decisions. Each node in the tree represents a feature, each branch represents a decision rule, and each leaf represents an outcome (e.g., malicious or benign).
- In Cybersecurity:
    - **Intrusion Detection:** Analyzing network traffic to identify malicious activity based on features like source/destination IP, port numbers, and protocols.
    - **Malware Detection:** Classifying files as malicious or benign based on features like API calls, file permissions, and code characteristics.

3. Random Forests
- **The Idea:** Random forests are an ensemble method that combines multiple decision trees. Each tree is trained on a different subset of the data and features, and the final prediction is made by aggregating the predictions of all the trees. This helps to improve accuracy and reduce overfitting.
- In Cybersecurity:
    - **Malware Detection:** Classifying files as malicious or benign based on a wide range of features.
    - **Intrusion Detection:** Identifying malicious network traffic by analyzing various network features.

Why These Algorithms Are Useful:
- **Interpretability:** Naive Bayes and decision trees are relatively easy to understand and interpret, making it easier to see why a particular decision was made.
- **Efficiency:** These algorithms are generally efficient and can handle large datasets.
- **Accuracy:** Random forests, in particular, can achieve high accuracy due to the ensemble approach.

Things to Keep in Mind:
- **Data is Crucial:** Supervised learning algorithms need labeled data to train effectively.
- **Feature Engineering:** Selecting and engineering relevant features is important for good performance.
- **Overfitting:** Decision trees can be prone to overfitting if not properly pruned.

In short: Naive Bayes is a simple and efficient algorithm for tasks like spam filtering, while decision trees provide a more interpretable approach to classification. Random forests combine the power of multiple decision trees to achieve high accuracy in complex cybersecurity tasks.

Deep learning models: Convolutional Neural Networks (CNNs) for image-based malware analysis

You're absolutely right to highlight Convolutional Neural Networks (CNNs) in the context of image-based malware analysis! They've proven to be very effective for this task. Here's why:

Why CNNs are a Good Fit:
- **Image Recognition:** CNNs are designed specifically for image processing. They excel at automatically learning spatial hierarchies of features in images, which is exactly what's needed when you represent malware as an image.
- **Malware Visualization:** Malware can be visualized as grayscale images where the pixel intensities correspond to the byte values of the malware's binary code. These images can reveal visual patterns and textures that are characteristic of different

malware families or behaviors.

- **Feature Extraction:** CNNs can automatically learn the most discriminative features from these malware images, such as textures, edges, and patterns, without the need for manual feature engineering.

How CNNs are Used for Malware Analysis:

1. **Malware Image Generation:** The binary code of a malware sample is converted into a grayscale image.
2. **CNN Model Training:** A CNN model is trained on a dataset of malware images with known labels (e.g., malware family or type). The CNN learns to associate visual patterns in the images with specific malware characteristics.
3. **Malware Classification:** Once trained, the CNN can be used to classify new, unseen malware samples by analyzing their image representations.

Benefits of CNNs for Image-Based Malware Analysis:

- **Automatic Feature Learning:** CNNs can automatically learn relevant features from malware images, eliminating the need for manual feature engineering.
- **High Accuracy:** CNNs can achieve high accuracy in malware classification, often outperforming traditional machine learning algorithms.
- **Robustness:** CNNs can be robust to variations in malware code, such as obfuscation and packing techniques.

Example:
Imagine a CNN being trained on images of different types of malware, like ransomware, spyware, and viruses. The CNN learns to recognize the unique visual patterns associated with each type of malware. When a new, unknown file is encountered, its image is generated and fed to the CNN. The CNN then classifies the file based on the visual patterns it has learned.
Key Considerations:

- **Dataset Size:** Training CNNs effectively requires a large and diverse dataset of malware images.
- **Computational Resources:** Training deep CNNs can be computationally intensive, requiring powerful hardware.
- **Evasion Techniques:** Malware developers may try to develop techniques to evade detection by manipulating the visual representation of malware.

Despite these challenges, CNNs have become a valuable tool in the fight against malware, enabling more accurate and efficient detection and classification of malicious software.

- Natural Language Processing (NLP):
    - **Sentiment analysis:** Analyzing security forums and social media for emerging threats.
    - **Topic modeling:** Identifying key themes and patterns in threat intelligence

reports:

Natural Language Processing (NLP) techniques like sentiment analysis and topic modelling can be applied to enhance cybersecurity:

1. Sentiment Analysis for Emerging Threats:
   - **The Idea:** Sentiment analysis aims to understand the emotional tone behind text. In cybersecurity, this means analyzing security forums, social media posts, and news articles to gauge public sentiment about potential threats.
   - **How it Works:** NLP algorithms are used to classify text as positive, negative, or neutral. More sophisticated approaches can even detect more nuanced emotions like fear, anger, or urgency.
   - In Cybersecurity:
     - **Early Warning System:** By monitoring social media and security forums, you can identify spikes in negative sentiment related to a specific product or service. This could indicate a developing vulnerability or exploit.
     - **Threat Intelligence:** Analyzing discussions about cyberattacks can provide insights into emerging threats, attack vectors, and attacker tactics.
     - **Reputation Management:** Sentiment analysis can help organizations understand how the public perceives their security posture and identify potential reputational risks.
     - **Example:** A sudden surge of negative tweets about a specific software's performance after an update could suggest a bug or a potential vulnerability being exploited.
2. Topic Modelling for Threat Intelligence:
   - **The Idea:** Topic modeling helps discover underlying topics in a collection of documents. In cybersecurity, this means analyzing threat intelligence reports, security blogs, and research papers to identify key themes and patterns.
   - **How it Works:** Algorithms like Latent Dirichlet Allocation (LDA) are used to identify groups of words that frequently occur together. These groups of words represent underlying topics.
   - In Cybersecurity:
     - **Threat Landscape Understanding:** Topic modeling can help security analysts understand the overall threat landscape by identifying prevalent attack techniques, malware types, and threat actors.
     - **Trend Analysis:** By analyzing changes in topic prevalence over time, you can identify emerging trends in cyberattacks.
     - **Knowledge Management:** Topic modeling can help organize and categorize threat intelligence information, making it easier to search and retrieve relevant information.
     - **Example:** Analyzing a collection of threat intelligence reports might reveal topics like "ransomware attacks targeting healthcare," "phishing campaigns using COVID-19 themes," or "exploits targeting IoT devices."

Benefits of Using NLP:

- **Scalability:** NLP can process large volumes of text data much faster than humans, making it possible to monitor vast amounts of information.
- **Automation:** NLP can automate many tasks, such as threat intelligence analysis and incident response.
- **Proactive Defense:** By identifying emerging threats early, NLP can help organizations take proactive steps to protect themselves.

Challenges:

- **Context Understanding:** NLP algorithms can sometimes struggle with understanding the context and nuances of human language.
- **Data Quality:** The accuracy of NLP results depends on the quality of the text data.
- **Bias:** NLP models can be biased if the training data is biased.

Despite these challenges, NLP is a powerful tool for enhancing cybersecurity. By combining sentiment analysis and topic modeling, organizations can gain valuable insights into the threat landscape and improve their ability to defend against cyberattacks.

Challenges and Considerations

Data quality and bias: Impact of biased data on AI/ML models Data quality and bias are critical concerns for AI/ML models in cybersecurity. Biased data can severely impact the performance and reliability of these models, leading to inaccurate predictions, unfair outcomes, and even security vulnerabilities. Here's a breakdown:

What is Biased Data?

Biased data occurs when the data used to train an AI/ML model doesn't accurately represent the real-world scenarios the model will encounter. This can manifest in several ways:

- **Sampling Bias:** The training data doesn't reflect the true distribution of different types of attacks or malware. For example, if a malware detection model is trained primarily on samples of common malware, it might fail to detect rarer but more sophisticated attacks.
- **Measurement Bias:** Errors or inconsistencies in how data is collected can introduce bias. For example, if network logs are incomplete or unreliable, the model might learn incorrect patterns.
- **Labeling Bias:** In supervised learning, incorrect or inconsistent labels in the training data can mislead the model. For example, if some malicious files are mistakenly labeled as benign, the model will learn to associate malicious features with benign files.
- **Temporal Bias:** Data collected over a specific time period might not be representative of future threats. Attack patterns and malware evolve, so a model trained on old data might be ineffective against new attacks.

Impact of Biased Data on AI/ML Models:

- **Reduced Accuracy:** A model trained on biased data will likely perform poorly on real-world data, leading to inaccurate predictions and missed threats.
- **Increased False Positives/Negatives:** Biased models can generate an excessive number of false positives (flagging benign activity as malicious) or false negatives (failing to detect malicious activity). This can overwhelm security teams and undermine trust in the AI/ML system.
- **Security Vulnerabilities:** A biased model might fail to detect certain types of attacks, creating security vulnerabilities that attackers can exploit.
- **Unfair or Discriminatory Outcomes:** In some cases, biased models can lead to unfair or discriminatory outcomes. For example, a user behavior analytics model trained on biased data might unfairly flag certain user groups as suspicious.
- **Lack of Trust:** If a model is known to be biased, users and security teams will be less likely to trust its predictions, limiting its effectiveness.

Mitigating Data Bias:

- **Data Collection and Preprocessing:** Carefully collect data from diverse sources and ensure that it is representative of real-world scenarios. Clean and preprocess the data to remove errors and inconsistencies.
- **Bias Detection:** Use techniques to identify and measure bias in the data.
- **Data Augmentation:** Augment the training data with synthetic data or by applying transformations to existing data to address imbalances.
- **Model Evaluation:** Evaluate the model's performance on a diverse set of test data to identify potential biases.
- **Explainable AI (XAI):** Use XAI techniques to understand how the model is making decisions and identify potential sources of bias.
- **Continuous Monitoring:** Continuously monitor the model's performance in real-world settings and retrain it with new data to address evolving threats and biases.

Addressing data quality and bias is essential for building effective and reliable AI/ML models in cybersecurity. By taking steps to mitigate bias, organizations can improve the accuracy, fairness, and trustworthiness of their AI/ML systems, leading to better security outcomes.

Explainability and interpretability: Understanding how AI/ML models make decisions

Explainability and interpretability are essential for building trust, ensuring accountability, and effectively using these powerful tools. Here's why they matter:

The Difference:

- **Explainability:** This focuses on *why* a model made a specific decision. It provides insights into the factors that led to a particular outcome.

- **Interpretability:** This is about *how* the model works. It aims to make the internal logic and mechanics of the model understandable to humans.

Why They Are Important in Cybersecurity:

- **Trust and Confidence:** Security analysts need to trust that the AI/ML system is making correct decisions.Explainability and interpretability help build this trust by showing how the model arrives at its conclusions.
- **Debugging and Improvement:** When a model makes a mistake, it's crucial to understand why. Explainability and interpretability make it easier to debug the model, identify biases, and improve its performance.
- **Compliance and Regulation:** Many industries have regulations that require transparency and accountability in decision-making processes, especially when sensitive data is involved. Explainable AI/ML can help meet these requirements.
- **Security Auditing:** Explainability allows for better auditing of AI/ML systems. This is important for identifying potential vulnerabilities, ensuring compliance, and investigating security incidents.
- **User Acceptance:** Security teams are more likely to adopt and use AI/ML tools if they understand how they work and can trust their decisions.

Challenges:

- **Complexity:** Many powerful AI/ML models, especially deep learning models, are complex "black boxes" that are difficult to interpret.
- **Trade-off:** There is often a trade-off between accuracy and interpretability. More complex models might be more accurate but less interpretable.
- **Lack of Standard Metrics:** There are no universally agreed-upon metrics for measuring explainability and interpretability.

Techniques for Enhancing Explainability and Interpretability:

- **Using Simpler Models:** Simpler models like decision trees or rule-based systems are often more interpretable than complex neural networks.
- **Feature Importance Analysis:** Techniques like SHAP values can help identify the most important features that contribute to a model's predictions.
- **Local Explanations:** Methods like LIME can provide explanations for individual predictions by approximating the complex model with a simpler, local model.
- **Visualization:** Visualizing the model's decision-making process can help humans understand how it works.

In Cybersecurity:

- **Malware Analysis:** Understanding why a model classifies a file as malware can help identify key characteristics of the malware and improve detection techniques.
- **Intrusion Detection:** Explaining why a network connection is flagged as suspicious

can help security analysts investigate the potential attack and take appropriate action.

- **User Behavior Analytics:** Understanding why a user's behavior is considered anomalous can help identify potential insider threats or compromised accounts.

Explainability and interpretability are critical for the responsible and effective use of AI/ML in cybersecurity. By focusing on these aspects, organizations can build more trustworthy, reliable, and accountable AI/ML systems that can significantly enhance their security posture

Adversarial attacks: Evasion techniques used by attackers to fool AI/ML models. Adversarial attacks are a significant threat to AI/ML models in cybersecurity. They involve carefully crafted inputs designed to "fool" the model, causing it to make incorrect predictions or misclassifications. These attacks exploit vulnerabilities in the model's learning process or the way it processes data. Here's a breakdown:

How Adversarial Attacks Work

The core idea is to make small, often imperceptible changes to the input data that drastically alter the model's output. Think of it like a camouflage that makes a threat invisible to the AI. Common Evasion Techniques:

- **Evasion Attacks (also known as adversarial examples):** These attacks modify legitimate inputs (like a file or network traffic) in a way that makes them misclassified by the model. For example:
    - **Malware:** Slightly altering the byte sequence of a malware file can make it undetectable by a machine learning classifier, even though its functionality remains unchanged.
    - **Phishing:** Adding subtle changes to a phishing email (like slightly altering URLs or adding invisible characters) can bypass detection algorithms.
    - **Image Recognition (relevant to malware image analysis):** Carefully crafted "noise" added to an image of malware can cause the CNN to misclassify it.
- **Poisoning Attacks:** These attacks target the training data itself. By injecting malicious or manipulated data into the training set, attackers can corrupt the model's learning process and cause it to make incorrect predictions on future inputs. This is a more insidious attack, as it can be harder to detect and can affect the model's performance over the long term.
- **Model Extraction Attacks:** These attacks aim to steal the model itself. By querying the model repeatedly, the attacker can gather enough information to create a copy of the model, which they can then use to develop evasion attacks or to gain insights into the organization's security strategies.

Impact of Adversarial Attacks

- **Bypassing Defenses:** Adversarial attacks can allow malware to evade detection, phishing emails to reach their targets, and malicious network activity to go unnoticed.

- **Compromising Integrity:** Poisoning attacks can compromise the integrity of the AI/ML system, making it unreliable for security tasks.
- **Data Breaches:** Successful adversarial attacks can lead to data breaches and other security incidents.
- **Erosion of Trust:** If AI/ML systems are vulnerable to adversarial attacks, it can erode trust in these technologies and limit their adoption in security-critical applications.

Defense Strategies

- **Adversarial Training:** This involves training the model on adversarial examples, making it more robust to these attacks.
- **Input Sanitization:** Techniques to detect and remove adversarial "noise" from inputs.
- **Robust Feature Engineering:** Designing features that are less susceptible to manipulation.
- **Model Hardening:** Techniques to make models more resistant to adversarial attacks.
- **Anomaly Detection:** Combining AI/ML models with anomaly detection systems to identify suspicious activities even if the model is fooled.
- **Regular Model Updates:** Keeping models up-to-date with the latest security patches and retraining them on new data.

Adversarial attacks are an ongoing challenge for AI/ML in cybersecurity. Defending against these attacks requires a multi-layered approach that combines robust model training, input validation, and continuous monitoring. It's an arms race, with attackers and defenders constantly developing new techniques.

Ethical considerations: Privacy, fairness, and accountability in AI/ML-powered security systems

Ethical considerations are paramount when deploying AI/ML-powered security systems. While these technologies offer tremendous potential, they also raise important questions about privacy, fairness, and accountability. Here's a breakdown:

1. Privacy:

- **Data Collection and Use:** AI/ML models often require vast amounts of data, including potentially sensitive information about users, systems, and network activity. It's crucial to collect only necessary data, use it responsibly, and ensure it is protected from unauthorized access. Anonymization and pseudonymization techniques can help mitigate privacy risks.
- **Inference and Profiling:** AI/ML models can infer sensitive information about individuals based on their behavior or network activity. This profiling can lead to privacy violations if not handled carefully. Transparency about how inferences are made is essential.
- **Data Retention:** Organizations need clear policies on how long they retain data used

for AI/ML systems and how they dispose of it securely.

2. Fairness:
   - **Bias in Training Data:** As discussed earlier, biased training data can lead to unfair or discriminatory outcomes. For example, a security system trained on biased data might unfairly flag certain user groups as suspicious. It's essential to identify and mitigate bias in data and models.
   - **Algorithmic Fairness:** Even with unbiased data, AI/ML algorithms themselves can introduce bias. It's important to evaluate models for fairness and ensure they don't discriminate against certain groups.
   - **Transparency and Explainability:** Understanding how a model makes decisions is crucial for ensuring fairness. Explainable AI/ML techniques can help identify potential biases and ensure that the system is making fair and equitable decisions.
3. Accountability:
   - **Responsibility for Decisions:** When an AI/ML system makes a mistake, it's important to determine who is responsible. Is it the developer of the model? The organization that deployed it? Clear lines of accountability are needed.
   - **Auditing and Monitoring:** AI/ML systems should be regularly audited and monitored to ensure they are working as intended and not causing unintended harm. This includes monitoring for bias, accuracy, and compliance with ethical guidelines.
   - **Transparency and Communication:** Organizations should be transparent about how they use AI/ML in security systems and communicate clearly with users about the potential impacts on their privacy and security.
   - **Human Oversight:** AI/ML systems should be subject to human oversight, especially in critical security decisions. Humans should have the ability to review and override the decisions made by AI/ML systems.

Best Practices for Ethical AI/ML in Cybersecurity

- **Develop Ethical Guidelines:** Establish clear ethical guidelines for the development and deployment of AI/ML systems.
- **Data Governance Framework:** Implement a robust data governance framework that addresses data collection, use, retention, and security.
- **Bias Detection and Mitigation:** Use techniques to identify and mitigate bias in data and models.
- **Explainable AI/ML:** Prioritize the use of explainable AI/ML techniques to ensure transparency and accountability.
- **Regular Audits and Monitoring:** Conduct regular audits and monitoring of AI/ML systems to ensure they are working as intended and not causing unintended harm.
- **Human-in-the-Loop:** Maintain human oversight of AI/ML systems, especially in critical security decisions.
- **Stakeholder Engagement:** Engage with stakeholders, including users, security teams, and policymakers, to discuss the ethical implications of AI/ML in cybersecurity.

By addressing these ethical considerations proactively, organizations can harness the power of AI/ML in cybersecurity responsibly and ensure that these technologies are used in a way that benefits society.

Future Directions

AI/ML-driven cybersecurity mesh: Integrating AI/ML across the entire security stack. An AI/ML-driven cybersecurity mesh represents a significant evolution in how we approach security. It's about weaving AI/ML capabilities throughout *all* layers of the security infrastructure, rather than just in isolated tools. This interconnected approach allows for more comprehensive threat detection, faster response, and a more adaptive security posture.

Here's what an AI/ML-driven cybersecurity mesh entails:

- **Integration Across the Stack:** AI/ML is embedded in various security components, including:
  - **Network Security:** AI-powered firewalls, intrusion detection/prevention systems, and network traffic analysis tools can identify anomalies and malicious activity in real-time.
  - **Endpoint Security:** AI-driven endpoint detection and response (EDR) solutions can detect and respond to malware, ransomware, and other endpoint threats.
  - **Data Security:** AI/ML can be used for data loss prevention (DLP), user behavior analytics (UBA), and access control, protecting sensitive data from unauthorized access or exfiltration.
  - **Cloud Security:** AI/ML can secure cloud environments by detecting anomalies in cloud workloads, identifying misconfigurations, and enforcing security policies.
  - **Identity and Access Management (IAM):** AI-powered IAM systems can detect and prevent unauthorized access by analyzing user behavior and identifying suspicious login attempts.
  - **Vulnerability Management:** AI/ML can prioritize vulnerabilities based on their exploitability and potential impact, helping security teams focus on the most critical issues.
  - **Threat Intelligence:** AI/ML can analyze threat intelligence feeds to identify emerging threats and predict future attacks.
  - **Security Orchestration, Automation, and Response (SOAR):** AI/ML can enhance SOAR capabilities by automating incident response workflows and improving decision-making.
- **Collaboration and Information Sharing:** The key to a mesh is that these AI/ML-powered components don't operate in silos. They share information and collaborate to provide a holistic view of the security landscape. For instance, an anomaly detected by the network security system could be correlated with suspicious activity on an endpoint to identify a coordinated attack.

- **Adaptive Security:** The mesh learns and adapts over time. As new threats emerge and attack techniques evolve, the AI/ML models are continuously updated and retrained to stay ahead of the curve.
- **Centralized Management and Visibility:** A central platform provides a unified view of the security posture, enabling security teams to monitor the effectiveness of the mesh and make informed decisions.

Benefits of a Cybersecurity Mesh:

- **Improved Threat Detection:** The interconnected nature of the mesh allows for more comprehensive threat detection, as threats can be identified at multiple layers of the security stack.
- **Faster Incident Response:** Automated incident response workflows enable organizations to respond quickly and effectively to security incidents.
- **Enhanced Security Posture:** The adaptive nature of the mesh helps organizations maintain a strong security posture in the face of evolving threats.
- **Reduced Complexity:** By integrating AI/ML across the security stack, organizations can simplify security management and reduce the complexity of their security infrastructure.

Challenges:

- **Integration:** Integrating AI/ML capabilities across the entire security stack can be complex and challenging.
- **Data Sharing:** Effective information sharing between different security components requires robust data sharing mechanisms.
- **Talent:** Building and maintaining an AI/ML-driven cybersecurity mesh requires skilled security professionals with expertise in AI/ML.

Despite these challenges, the AI/ML-driven cybersecurity mesh represents the future of security. By weaving AI/ML throughout the security infrastructure, organizations can achieve a more comprehensive, adaptive, and effective defense against cyber threats.

AI/ML for proactive security: Predictive threat intelligence and automated incident response AI/ML is transforming cybersecurity from a reactive posture to a proactive one, particularly through predictive threat intelligence and automated incident response. Here's how:

1. Predictive Threat Intelligence:

- **The Challenge:** Traditional threat intelligence often focuses on past attacks. AI/ML can shift this to *predicting*future attacks.
- How AI/ML Helps:
    - **Analyzing Historical Data:** AI/ML algorithms can analyze vast amounts of historical attack data (malware samples, attack patterns, vulnerabilities exploited) to identify trends and predict future attack vectors.

- **Monitoring Threat Landscape:** AI/ML can monitor threat intelligence feeds, social media, and other sources to identify emerging threats and assess their potential impact.
- **Behavioral Analysis:** AI/ML can analyze user and system behavior to identify anomalies that may indicate an impending attack.

- Benefits:
    - **Proactive Defense:** Organizations can take proactive steps to patch vulnerabilities, strengthen defenses, and prepare for potential attacks *before* they occur.
    - **Resource Allocation:** Predictive threat intelligence helps prioritize security efforts and allocate resources effectively.
    - **Improved Situational Awareness:** Provides a better understanding of the evolving threat landscape.

2. Automated Incident Response:
    - **The Challenge:** Responding to security incidents manually is often slow and resource-intensive.
    - How AI/ML Helps:
        - **Automated Threat Detection:** AI/ML can automatically detect security incidents, such as malware infections, phishing attacks, and network intrusions.
        - **Automated Triage and Analysis:** AI/ML can automatically triage and analyze security alerts, prioritizing the most critical incidents.
        - **Automated Containment and Remediation:** AI/ML can automate containment measures, such as isolating infected systems, blocking malicious traffic, and disabling compromised accounts. It can also automate remediation steps, such as patching vulnerabilities and removing malware.
    - Benefits:
        - **Faster Response Times:** Automated incident response significantly reduces the time it takes to respond to security incidents, minimizing the impact of attacks.
        - **Reduced Human Error:** Automation reduces the risk of human error in incident response.
        - **Improved Efficiency:** Automated incident response frees up security analysts to focus on more complex tasks.

Synergies: Predictive threat intelligence and automated incident response work together synergistically. Predictive intelligence can inform automated response workflows, enabling them to anticipate and proactively mitigate potential threats. For example, if the system predicts a high likelihood of a phishing attack targeting a specific group of employees, it can automatically deploy enhanced phishing awareness training to those employees.

Key Considerations:

- **Accuracy of Predictions:** Predictive threat intelligence is not perfect. It's essential to validate predictions and avoid over-reliance on them.
- **Human Oversight:** While automation is crucial, human oversight is still necessary, especially for complex or unusual incidents.
- **Integration:** Effective AI/ML-driven proactive security requires seamless integration between different security tools and systems.

By combining predictive threat intelligence and automated incident response, organizations can create a more proactive and resilient security posture, enabling them to anticipate and effectively respond to evolving cyber threats.

The role of AI/ML in developing more resilient and secure systems

AI/ML is playing a critical role in building more resilient and secure systems in cybersecurity. Here's how:

1. Enhanced Threat Detection:
    - **Anomaly Detection:** AI/ML algorithms can analyze vast amounts of data to identify subtle anomalies that might indicate a cyberattack. This includes unusual network traffic, user behavior, or system activity.
    - **Malware Detection:** AI/ML models can be trained to recognize patterns and characteristics of malware, even new or polymorphic variants, enabling more accurate and efficient malware detection.
    - **Phishing Detection:** AI/ML can analyze email content, sender information, and links to identify phishing attempts with high accuracy.
    - **Intrusion Detection:** AI/ML can analyze network traffic and system logs to detect intrusions in real-time, even those that evade traditional signature-based systems.
2. Proactive Security:
    - **Predictive Threat Intelligence:** AI/ML can analyze historical attack data and threat intelligence feeds to predict future attacks and proactively strengthen defenses.
    - **Vulnerability Prioritization:** AI/ML can prioritize vulnerabilities based on their exploitability and potential impact, helping security teams focus on the most critical issues.
    - **Automated Security Hardening:** AI/ML can automate security hardening tasks, such as patching vulnerabilities, configuring firewalls, and enforcing security policies.
3. Faster Incident Response:
    - **Automated Threat Detection and Alerting:** AI/ML can automatically detect security incidents and generate alerts, enabling security teams to respond quickly.
    - **Automated Incident Triage and Analysis:** AI/ML can automatically triage and analyze security alerts, prioritizing the most critical incidents.

- **Automated Containment and Remediation:** AI/ML can automate containment measures, such as isolating infected systems, blocking malicious traffic, and disabling compromised accounts.

4. Adaptive Security:
   - **Continuous Learning:** AI/ML models can continuously learn from new data and adapt to evolving threats, ensuring that security systems remain effective over time.
   - **Dynamic Security Policies:** AI/ML can enable dynamic security policies that adapt to changing conditions and user behavior.
5. Improved Security Automation:
   - **Automated Security Tasks:** AI/ML can automate many routine security tasks, such as log analysis, vulnerability scanning, and security testing.
   - **Security Orchestration and Automation:** AI/ML can enhance security orchestration and automation platforms by enabling more intelligent and adaptive workflows.

Overall Benefits:

- **Increased Resilience:** AI/ML helps build more resilient systems that can withstand cyberattacks and recover quickly.
- **Reduced Risk:** By proactively identifying and mitigating threats, AI/ML helps reduce the risk of security breaches and data loss.
- **Improved Efficiency:** AI/ML automates security tasks, freeing up security teams to focus on more strategic initiatives.
- **Enhanced Security Posture:** AI/ML enables organizations to maintain a strong security posture in the face of evolving threats.

Key Considerations:

- **Data Quality and Bias:** AI/ML models are only as good as the data they are trained on. It's crucial to ensure data quality and address potential biases.
- **Explainability and Interpretability:** Understanding how AI/ML models make decisions is essential for building trust and ensuring accountability.
- **Adversarial Attacks:** AI/ML models can be vulnerable to adversarial attacks. It's important to develop defenses against these attacks.
- **Ethical Considerations:** The use of AI/ML in cybersecurity raises ethical concerns, such as privacy, fairness, and accountability.

Despite these challenges, AI/ML is a powerful tool for building more resilient and secure systems. By leveraging the power of AI/ML, organizations can significantly improve their ability to defend against cyber threats and protect their valuable assets.

Conclusion

Recap of the key benefits and challenges of AI/ML in cybersecurity. Emphasizing the importance of responsible and ethical development and deployment of AI/ML in security. **Call to action:** Encourage further research and collaboration to advance the field of AI/ML in cybersecurity. AI/ML has emerged as a transformative force in cybersecurity, offering immense potential to enhance our defenses against increasingly sophisticated cyber threats. We've explored how AI/ML empowers us with enhanced threat detection through anomaly detection, malware and phishing classification, and intrusion detection. It enables proactive security through predictive threat intelligence and automated security hardening, and accelerates incident response with automated threat detection, triage, and remediation. Furthermore, AI/ML fosters adaptive security systems that continuously learn and evolve, and improves overall security automation. However, this powerful technology comes with its own set of challenges. We must be mindful of data quality and potential biases that can skew results. Explainability and interpretability are crucial for building trust and ensuring accountability. Adversarial attacks pose a serious threat, requiring constant vigilance and innovative defense strategies. And perhaps most importantly, we must grapple with the ethical considerations surrounding privacy, fairness, and accountability in AI/ML-driven security systems. The responsible and ethical development and deployment of AI/ML in security is not just a best practice—it's a necessity. We must prioritize data privacy, ensure fairness in our algorithms, and establish clear lines of accountability. Transparency and explainability are key to building trust and ensuring that these powerful tools are used for good.

3

Blockchain and Cybersecurity

During the early half of the last decade, blockchain was still a very nascent technology. Cryptocurrency - probably and arguably the most important thing to come out of the blockchain ecosystem was just mushrooming in its early days. At a time like, I got to oversee the development of Blockchain at organizations like Google, IBM, Adobe and Apple during different interactions with these companies, around projects, research work and developer conferences where I presented often. Thus, I have tried to provide a very different view of the Blockchain industry and how it interacts with cybersecurity so that you – the reader – are able to get a very holistic and birds eye view of this industry – and apply the knowledge learnt here through actionable insights towards building a very solid foundation for a career at the intersection of blockchain, quantum computing and cybersecurity.

Brief Overview of Blockchain Technology

Blockchain is a distributed, immutable ledger that records transactions in a chain of interconnected "blocks." Each block contains a timestamp, transaction data, and a cryptographic hash of the previous block, creating a secure and tamper-proof record.

- **Decentralization:** Blockchain data is distributed across a network of computers, rather than stored in a single location. This makes it resistant to single points of failure and censorship.
- **Immutability:** Once a block is added to the chain, it cannot be altered or deleted without changing all subsequent blocks. This ensures the integrity and trustworthiness of the data.
- **Transparency:** Most blockchains are transparent, meaning that all transactions are publicly viewable. This enhances accountability and auditability.

Types of Blockchains

- **Public Blockchains:** Anyone can participate in the network, validate transactions, and view the ledger (e.g., Bitcoin, Ethereum).
- **Private Blockchains:** Access to the network is restricted to authorized participants, often within a single organization.
- **Permissioned Blockchains:** A hybrid approach where access is controlled, but the

network may be managed by multiple organizations.

Key Applications Beyond Cryptocurrency

- **Supply Chain Management:** Tracking goods from origin to consumer, ensuring authenticity and transparency.
- **Healthcare:** Securely storing and sharing patient medical records, improving interoperability and patient control.
- **Finance:** Streamlining financial transactions, reducing costs, and improving security.
- **Voting Systems:** Creating tamper-proof and transparent voting systems.
- **Digital Identity:** Providing individuals with secure and verifiable digital identities.
- **IoT Security:** Securing communication and data exchange between IoT devices.

Blockchain's Relevance to Cybersecurity

Blockchain's inherent features offer several potential benefits for cybersecurity:

- **Data Integrity:** Immutability ensures that data stored on the blockchain cannot be tampered with, enhancing trust and security.
- **Decentralization:** Reduces the risk of single points of failure and data breaches.
- **Transparency:** Enhances auditability and accountability.
- **Identity Management:** Blockchain can be used to create secure and verifiable digital identities, reducing the risk of identity theft.
- **Secure Data Sharing:** Blockchain enables secure and controlled data sharing between authorized parties.
- **Supply Chain Security:** Tracking products throughout the supply chain can help identify counterfeit goods and prevent tampering.

While blockchain is not a silver bullet for all cybersecurity problems, it offers a powerful set of tools for enhancing security and building more resilient systems. It's important to note that blockchain itself can be vulnerable to attacks, so proper security measures are still necessary.

Cybersecurity challenges in the digital age

- Data breaches, ransomware attacks, phishing scams.
- The rise of IoT devices and the increasing attack surface.
- The need for more secure and resilient systems

The most pressing cybersecurity challenges we face in today's digital age. Let's break them down:

- **Data Breaches:** These incidents involve unauthorized access and exfiltration of sensitive data, whether it's personal information, financial records, intellectual property, or trade secrets. Data breaches can have devastating consequences for individuals and organizations, including financial losses, reputational damage, legal liabilities, and loss of customer trust. The sheer volume of data being generated and stored makes it a prime target.

- **Ransomware Attacks:** Ransomware has become a pervasive and highly damaging threat. Attackers encrypt an organization's data or systems and demand a ransom payment in exchange for the decryption key. These attacks can cripple businesses, disrupt critical services (like healthcare), and cause significant financial losses. The increasing sophistication of ransomware and the rise of "double extortion" (stealing data before encrypting it) make this threat even more challenging.
- **Phishing Scams:** Phishing remains one of the most common and effective attack vectors. These scams use deceptive emails, messages, or websites to trick individuals into revealing sensitive information, such as passwords, credit card numbers, or login credentials. Phishing attacks are constantly evolving, becoming more sophisticated and personalized, making them harder to detect. They exploit human psychology and trust.
- **The Rise of IoT Devices:** The proliferation of Internet of Things (IoT) devices has dramatically expanded the attack surface. From smart home appliances to industrial control systems, these devices often have weak security and can be easily compromised. They can be used as entry points for attackers to gain access to larger networks or to launch DDoS attacks. The sheer number and diversity of IoT devices make them a significant security challenge.
- **The Need for More Secure and Resilient Systems:** The challenges mentioned above underscore the critical need for more secure and resilient systems. This requires a multi-layered approach that includes:
    - **Stronger Authentication:** Multi-factor authentication, biometric authentication, and other advanced authentication methods.
    - **Data Encryption:** Protecting sensitive data both in transit and at rest.
    - **Security Awareness Training:** Educating users about cybersecurity best practices and how to recognize and avoid threats.
    - **Vulnerability Management:** Regularly scanning for and patching vulnerabilities in software and systems.
    - **Incident Response Planning:** Developing and testing incident response plans to ensure that organizations can effectively respond to security incidents.
    - **Zero Trust Security:** A security framework based on the principle of "never trust, always verify," which assumes that no user or device is inherently trusted.
    - **AI/ML Integration:** Leveraging AI/ML for threat detection, anomaly detection, and automated incident response.

In the face of these evolving cybersecurity challenges, organizations and individuals must adopt a proactive and comprehensive approach to security. This includes staying informed about the latest threats, implementing strong security measures, and fostering a culture of security awareness.

Blockchain's Role in Enhancing Cybersecurity

Blockchain technology, with its inherent characteristics of decentralization, immutability, and transparency, offers a unique set of tools to enhance cybersecurity in several ways:

1. Data Integrity and Immutability:
   - **How it helps:** Blockchain's immutability ensures that once data is recorded, it cannot be altered or tampered with.This is crucial for maintaining the integrity of security logs, audit trails, and other critical security information.
   - **Example:** Imagine a security system that logs all network events on a blockchain. Any attempt to modify these logs to hide malicious activity would be immediately detectable.
2. Decentralization and Resilience:
   - **How it helps:** Traditional centralized security systems have a single point of failure. If that point is compromised, the entire system is vulnerable. Blockchain's decentralized nature distributes data and control across a network, making it more resilient to attacks.
   - **Example:** A decentralized identity management system built on blockchain would be more resistant to large-scale data breaches compared to a centralized system.
3. Enhanced Identity and Access Management:
   - **How it helps:** Blockchain can be used to create secure and verifiable digital identities. This can help prevent identity theft and unauthorized access to systems and data.
   - **Example:** A blockchain-based system could allow users to control their own digital identities and grant access to specific services without relying on a central authority.
4. Secure Data Sharing and Collaboration:
   - **How it helps:** Blockchain can enable secure and controlled data sharing between organizations. This is particularly useful in situations where multiple parties need to collaborate on security-related tasks, such as threat intelligence sharing.
   - **Example:** Organizations could share threat intelligence data on a blockchain, ensuring that the information is authentic and hasn't been tampered with.
5. Supply Chain Security:
   - **How it helps:** Blockchain can be used to track products and materials throughout the supply chain, ensuring authenticity and preventing counterfeiting. This is important for securing critical infrastructure and preventing the introduction of compromised components.
   - **Example:** Tracking software updates on a blockchain could ensure that only legitimate updates are installed on devices, preventing malware from being introduced through compromised updates.
6. Securing IoT Devices:
   - **How it helps:** IoT devices often have limited processing power and security capabilities, making them vulnerable to attacks. Blockchain can provide a secure platform for managing and authenticating IoT devices, improving their overall

security.

- **Example:** A blockchain-based system could be used to manage the identities of IoT devices and secure their communication with each other.

Important Considerations:

- **Blockchain is not a silver bullet:** While blockchain offers several security benefits, it's not a complete solution to all cybersecurity challenges. It should be used in conjunction with other security measures.
- **Blockchain itself can be vulnerable:** Blockchain systems can be vulnerable to attacks, such as 51% attacks or smart contract vulnerabilities. It's crucial to implement appropriate security measures to protect blockchain systems themselves.
- **Scalability and Performance:** Blockchain technology can be slow and resource-intensive, which can limit its applicability in some security scenarios.

Despite these challenges, blockchain has the potential to play a significant role in enhancing cybersecurity. By leveraging its unique characteristics, organizations can build more secure and resilient systems to protect against evolving cyber threats.

Data Integrity and Immutability:

- Preventing data tampering and ensuring data authenticity.
- Applications in digital evidence, record keeping, and supply chain management.

Data integrity and immutability are foundational security principles, and blockchain offers a powerful way to achieve them. Let's delve into how these concepts, enhanced by blockchain, are crucial for cybersecurity:

Data Integrity and Immutability Explained

- **Data Integrity:** Ensures that data is accurate, complete, and consistent. It means that data hasn't been altered or corrupted in any unauthorized way.
- **Immutability:** Guarantees that once data is recorded, it cannot be changed or deleted. This creates a permanent and auditable record.

How Blockchain Enhances Data Integrity and Immutability

Blockchain's structure, with its linked blocks and cryptographic hashing, makes it exceptionally well-suited for ensuring data integrity and immutability:

1. **Cryptographic Hashing:** Each block in the blockchain contains a unique cryptographic hash of its contents. Any alteration to the data within a block will change its hash.
2. **Linked Blocks:** Each block also contains the hash of the *previous* block. This creates a chain of blocks, where each block is cryptographically linked to the one before it. If someone tries to tamper with a block, the hash of that block changes, *and* the hash in the following block becomes invalid, immediately revealing the tampering.

3. **Distributed Ledger:** The blockchain is distributed across many nodes in a network. This makes it extremely difficult for an attacker to tamper with the data, as they would need to control a majority of the nodes simultaneously.

Applications in Cybersecurity

- **Digital Evidence:** Blockchain can be used to create a tamper-proof record of digital evidence, ensuring its admissibility in legal proceedings. For example, timestamps and hashes of files or network activity can be recorded on the blockchain.
- **Record Keeping:** Securely storing critical records on a blockchain ensures their integrity and prevents unauthorized modifications. This is important for regulatory compliance and internal audits. Examples include:
  - Security logs: Maintaining an immutable log of security events.
  - Vulnerability reports: Tracking vulnerability scan results and remediation efforts.
  - Incident response records: Documenting incident details and actions taken.
- **Supply Chain Management:** Tracking products and materials on a blockchain can help prevent counterfeiting, ensure product authenticity, and improve supply chain transparency. This has security implications, for instance, in ensuring that software updates are genuine and haven't been tampered with.
- **Securing IoT Devices:** Blockchain can be used to manage the identities and data generated by IoT devices, ensuring that the data is authentic and hasn't been manipulated. This is crucial for securing critical infrastructure and preventing IoT-based attacks.
- **DNS Security:** Blockchain-based DNS systems can be more resistant to DNS spoofing and other attacks that redirect users to malicious websites.
- **Vulnerability Disclosure:** A secure, transparent, and immutable platform for vulnerability disclosure can improve security by allowing researchers to report vulnerabilities without fear of reprisal and ensuring that vendors are aware of the issues.

Benefits

- **Trust:** Blockchain's inherent properties build trust in the data.
- **Auditability:** The immutable record facilitates audits and investigations.
- **Accountability:** Changes to data can be easily traced back to their source.

Challenges

- **Scalability:** Blockchain can be slow and resource-intensive, which can limit its applicability in some situations.
- **Complexity:** Implementing blockchain-based security solutions can be complex.
- **Regulation:** The regulatory landscape surrounding blockchain is still evolving.

Despite these challenges, the ability to ensure data integrity and immutability is one of blockchain's most valuable contributions to cybersecurity. As the technology matures, we can expect to see even more innovative applications in this space.

Enhanced Trust and Transparency

- Building trust in digital transactions and interactions.
- Improving auditability and accountability.

You're right to point out the crucial role of trust and transparency in cybersecurity, and how blockchain can be a valuable tool in achieving those goals. Here's how blockchain contributes:

1. Building Trust in Digital Transactions and Interactions:

- **Transparency:** Blockchain's transparent nature allows all participants in a network to view the same record of transactions. This shared view builds trust, as there's no single party controlling the information.
- **Immutability:** The fact that blockchain records are immutable means that once a transaction is recorded, it cannot be altered or deleted. This provides a high level of assurance that the information is accurate and reliable.
- **Decentralization:** By distributing the ledger across a network, blockchain eliminates the need to trust a central authority. This reduces the risk of manipulation or censorship.

Examples

- **Supply Chain:** Consumers can trust that products are authentic and ethically sourced by tracing their journey on a blockchain.
- **Voting:** Transparent and immutable voting records on a blockchain can increase trust in election results.
- **Digital Identity:** Individuals can control their own digital identities and selectively share information with trusted parties, reducing the risk of identity theft.

2. Improving Auditability and Accountability in Cybersecurity

- **Immutable Audit Trails:** Blockchain can be used to create tamper-proof audit trails of security events, making it easier to investigate security incidents and identify the responsible parties.
- **Enhanced Accountability:** By providing a clear and transparent record of actions, blockchain can increase accountability for security-related decisions.
- **Streamlined Compliance:** Blockchain can simplify compliance with regulations that require organizations to maintain detailed records of security-related activities.

Examples

- **Incident Response:** Blockchain-based audit trails can help security teams understand the sequence of events during a cyberattack and identify the root cause.
- **Vulnerability Management:** Tracking vulnerability scans and remediation efforts on a blockchain can improve accountability and ensure that vulnerabilities are addressed

promptly.
- **Data Governance:** Blockchain can be used to record data access and usage, improving transparency and accountability in data governance.

Benefits
- **Increased Confidence:** Trust and transparency in digital interactions lead to increased confidence in systems and processes.
- **Reduced Fraud:** Immutability and transparency make it more difficult to commit fraud or manipulate data.
- **Improved Efficiency:** Blockchain can streamline audits and compliance processes, saving time and resources.

Challenges
- **Scalability:** Blockchain technology can be slow and resource-intensive, which can limit its applicability in some situations.
- **Privacy:** While blockchain can enhance transparency, it's important to ensure that sensitive data is protected.
- **Regulation:** The regulatory landscape surrounding blockchain is still evolving.

Despite these challenges, the ability to enhance trust and transparency is one of blockchain's most valuable contributions to cybersecurity. As the technology matures, we can expect to see even more innovative applications in this space.

Decentralized Identity Management
- Empowering individuals to control their own digital identities.
- Reducing reliance on centralized authorities.

Decentralized Identity Management (DID) is a game-changer in cybersecurity, and blockchain is a key enabler. Here's why and how:

The Problem with Centralized Identity
Traditional identity management relies on centralized authorities (like companies or governments) to store and manage our digital identities. This creates several vulnerabilities:

- **Single Point of Failure:** If the central authority is compromised, all user identities are at risk.
- **Data Breaches:** Centralized databases are attractive targets for hackers, leading to massive data breaches.
- **Lack of Control:** Users have limited control over their own data and how it is used.

How DID Solves These Problems

DID empowers individuals to take control of their digital identities by:

- **Decentralization:** Identity information is not stored in a central database but distributed across a network (often a blockchain).
- **Self-Sovereignty:** Users create and manage their own digital identities, independent of any central authority.
- **Privacy:** Users can selectively share information with trusted parties, limiting the amount of personal data exposed.

Key Components of DID

- **Decentralized Identifiers (DIDs):** Unique identifiers that are owned and controlled by the user.
- **Verifiable Credentials (VCs):** Digital credentials issued by trusted entities (like governments or universities) that can be verified without relying on the issuer.
- **Digital Wallets:** Secure applications where users store and manage their DIDs and VCs.

Benefits of DID in Cybersecurity

- **Reduced Risk of Data Breaches:** Decentralized storage makes it harder for hackers to steal large amounts of identity data.
- **Improved Privacy:** Users have greater control over their data and can limit what information they share.
- **Enhanced Security:** Cryptographic techniques are used to secure and verify identities.
- **Increased Trust:** DID enables trustless interactions, as users can verify credentials without relying on a central authority.
- **Interoperability:** DID can enable seamless interoperability between different systems and platforms.

Examples of DID Applications

- **Passwordless Authentication:** Users can authenticate to websites and applications using their DID, eliminating the need for passwords.
- **Secure Data Sharing:** Individuals can securely share personal information with healthcare providers, financial institutions, or other parties without relying on intermediaries.
- **Digital Signatures:** DID can be used to create digital signatures, ensuring the authenticity and integrity of documents.
- **IoT Device Management:** DID can be used to manage the identities of IoT devices, improving their security and interoperability.

Challenges and Considerations

- **Usability:** Making DID user-friendly is crucial for widespread adoption.
- **Scalability:** DID systems need to be able to handle large numbers of users and

transactions.

- **Regulation:** The regulatory landscape surrounding DID is still evolving.

Despite these challenges, DID has the potential to revolutionize how we manage digital identities, enhancing security, privacy, and user control. By reducing our reliance on centralized authorities, DID can make the internet a safer and more trustworthy place.

Secure Communication and Data Sharing

- Enabling secure and private data sharing among multiple parties.
- Applications in healthcare, finance, and government

Here we highlight the importance of secure communication and data sharing, especially in sensitive sectors like healthcare, finance, and government. Blockchain offers some compelling solutions in this area. Here's how:

The Challenge

Traditional methods of data sharing often involve centralized databases or intermediaries, creating vulnerabilities and privacy risks. These systems can be single points of failure, susceptible to breaches, and can give intermediaries excessive control over sensitive data.

How Blockchain Helps

Blockchain's decentralized, immutable, and transparent nature provides a strong foundation for secure communication and data sharing:

- **Decentralized Data Sharing:** Blockchain enables data sharing without relying on a central authority. This reduces the risk of data breaches and single points of failure.
- **Controlled Access:** Blockchain allows for fine-grained control over who can access specific data. Permissions can be managed securely using cryptographic techniques.
- **Auditable Data Sharing:** All data sharing transactions are recorded on the blockchain, creating a transparent and auditable record. This enhances accountability and helps ensure compliance with regulations.
- **Secure Communication Channels:** Blockchain can be used to establish secure communication channels between parties, protecting data in transit.

Applications in Cybersecurity

- Healthcare:
    - Securely sharing patient medical records between healthcare providers, improving interoperability and patient care while maintaining privacy.
    - Managing clinical trials data securely and transparently.
    - Tracking pharmaceuticals throughout the supply chain to prevent counterfeiting.
- Finance

    - Facilitating secure and efficient cross-border payments.
    - Sharing KYC (Know Your Customer) information securely between financial institutions.
    - Reducing fraud and improving transparency in financial transactions.
- Government
    - Securely sharing citizen data between government agencies.
    - Managing digital identities and credentials for citizens.
    - Improving transparency and accountability in government operations.
- Supply Chain Management (relevant to all sectors)
    - Tracking products and materials throughout the supply chain to prevent counterfeiting and ensure authenticity.
    - Sharing supply chain data securely with partners and stakeholders.
- Secure Messaging
    - Building secure messaging platforms that protect user privacy and prevent eavesdropping.

Specific Cybersecurity Benefits

- **Data Integrity:** Blockchain's immutability ensures that shared data hasn't been tampered with.
- **Confidentiality:** Encryption and access control mechanisms can be used to protect the confidentiality of shared data.
- **Non-Repudiation:** Blockchain can provide evidence of data sharing transactions, preventing parties from denying that they shared or received data.

Challenges and Considerations

- **Scalability:** Blockchain can be slow and resource-intensive, which can limit its applicability in some situations.
- **Privacy Concerns (ironically):** While blockchain can enhance privacy, it's important to carefully consider how data is stored and shared to avoid unintentionally revealing sensitive information. Techniques like zero-knowledge proofs can help address this.
- **Interoperability:** Ensuring interoperability between different blockchain platforms is crucial for widespread adoption.
- **Regulation:** The regulatory landscape surrounding blockchain and data sharing is still evolving.

Despite these challenges, blockchain offers a powerful set of tools for enabling secure communication and data sharing. As the technology matures, we can expect to see even more innovative applications in cybersecurity and other sectors.

Blockchain-Based Cybersecurity Solutions

Here we will understand how blockchain can be used to build concrete cybersecurity solutions. Here are some key areas where blockchain is making a difference:

1. Decentralized Identity Management (DID)
    - **Problem:** Traditional identity systems rely on centralized authorities, creating single points of failure and privacy risks.
    - **Solution:** Blockchain-based DID solutions empower individuals to control their own digital identities. Users create and manage their identities (using Decentralized Identifiers - DIDs) and selectively share verifiable credentials (VCs) with services, reducing reliance on central authorities and improving privacy.
    - **Example:** A user can prove their age to a website without revealing their birthdate, or grant a healthcare provider access to specific medical records without sharing their entire medical history.
2. Secure Data Sharing and Collaboration
    - **Problem:** Sharing sensitive data between organizations is often complex and risky, with concerns about data breaches and unauthorized access.
    - **Solution:** Blockchain enables secure and auditable data sharing between multiple parties. Data can be encrypted and access permissions managed on the blockchain, ensuring only authorized parties can access specific information.
    - **Example:** Healthcare providers can securely share patient medical records for collaborative care, or financial institutions can share KYC (Know Your Customer) information to combat money laundering.

3. Supply Chain Security
    - **Problem:** Supply chains are vulnerable to counterfeiting, tampering, and fraud, which can have significant security implications.
    - **Solution:** Blockchain can be used to track products and materials throughout the supply chain, from origin to consumer. This ensures authenticity, prevents counterfeiting, and improves transparency.
    - **Example:** Tracking pharmaceuticals on a blockchain can help prevent counterfeit drugs from entering the market, or verifying the origin of components in critical infrastructure can prevent the introduction of compromised parts.

4. Secure Voting Systems
    - **Problem:** Traditional voting systems can be vulnerable to manipulation and fraud, undermining public trust in elections.
    - **Solution:** Blockchain can be used to create transparent and tamper-proof voting systems. Each vote is recorded as a transaction on the blockchain, ensuring that votes cannot be altered or deleted.
    - **Example:** Estonia has been a pioneer in using blockchain for secure online voting, allowing citizens to vote remotely with confidence in the integrity of the process.
5. Securing IoT Devices
    - **Problem:** IoT devices often have limited processing power and security capabilities,

making them vulnerable to attacks.

- **Solution:** Blockchain can provide a secure platform for managing and authenticating IoT devices. Each device can have a unique identity on the blockchain, and secure communication channels can be established between devices.
- **Example:** Managing the identities and access control of smart home devices, industrial sensors, or connected vehicles on a blockchain can improve their security and prevent them from being compromised.

6. Decentralized DNS (Domain Name System)

- **Problem:** Traditional DNS systems are centralized and vulnerable to attacks like DNS spoofing, which can redirect users to malicious websites.
- **Solution:** Blockchain-based DNS systems distribute DNS records across a network, making them more resistant to attacks and censorship.
- **Example:** A decentralized DNS system can prevent attackers from hijacking domain names and redirecting users to phishing websites.

7. Secure Software Updates

- **Problem:** Software updates can be a vector for malware if they are compromised or come from untrusted sources.
- **Solution:** Blockchain can be used to ensure the authenticity and integrity of software updates. Software developers can sign updates with their private keys and record the updates on the blockchain, allowing users to verify that the updates are legitimate.
- **Example:** A blockchain-based system can ensure that only authorized updates are installed on devices, preventing malware from being introduced through compromised updates.

Important Considerations

- **Scalability:** Blockchain technology can be slow and resource-intensive, which can limit its applicability in some situations.
- **Security of the Blockchain itself:** While blockchain offers many security benefits, it is not immune to attacks. It's crucial to implement proper security measures to protect blockchain systems themselves.
- **Regulation:** The regulatory landscape surrounding blockchain is still evolving, and organizations need to be aware of the legal and regulatory implications of using blockchain-based solutions.

Despite these challenges, blockchain has the potential to play a significant role in enhancing cybersecurity. By leveraging its unique characteristics, organizations can build more secure and resilient systems to protect against evolving cyber threats.

Secure Data Storage and Sharing:

- Decentralized storage solutions (IPFS, Filecoin).

Confidential transactions and privacy-preserving techniques: secure data storage and sharing, as it's a critical aspect of cybersecurity, and blockchain offers some innovative solutions. Let's break it down:

The Challenge

Traditional centralized data storage and sharing methods are vulnerable to data breaches, single points of failure, and lack of transparency. This is especially problematic when dealing with sensitive information in sectors like healthcare, finance, and government.

How Blockchain Helps

Blockchain's unique characteristics can address these challenges:

- **Decentralized Storage:** Blockchain can be used to create decentralized storage solutions, where data is distributed across a network of nodes rather than stored in a single location. This makes it much harder for attackers to steal or tamper with data.
    - **Examples:** IPFS (Interplanetary File System) and Filecoin are examples of decentralized storage solutions that leverage blockchain technology. IPFS uses a content-addressed system, where files are identified by their content rather than their location, making them more resistant to censorship and tampering. Filecoin adds a blockchain-based incentive layer, allowing users to earn cryptocurrency by providing storage space to the network.
- **Secure Data Sharing:** Blockchain allows for fine-grained control over who can access specific data. Permissions can be managed securely using cryptographic techniques, ensuring that only authorized parties can access sensitive information.
    - **Examples:** In healthcare, blockchain can enable secure sharing of patient medical records between healthcare providers while preserving patient privacy. In finance, blockchain can facilitate secure sharing of KYC (Know Your Customer) information between financial institutions to combat money laundering.
- **Confidential Transactions:** Blockchain can be used to conduct confidential transactions, where the details of the transaction are encrypted and only visible to authorized parties. This is crucial for protecting sensitive financial information or personal data.
    - **Examples:** Techniques like zero-knowledge proofs allow for verifying that a transaction is valid without revealing any details about the transaction itself. This can be used to protect the privacy of financial transactions or to verify identity information without revealing the underlying data.
- **Privacy-Preserving Techniques:** Blockchain can be combined with other privacy-enhancing technologies (PETs) to further protect sensitive data.
    - **Examples:** Techniques like homomorphic encryption allow for performing computations on encrypted data without decrypting it, enabling data analysis while preserving privacy. Secure multi-party computation (MPC) allows

multiple parties to collaborate on computations without revealing their individual data.

Specific Cybersecurity Benefits

- **Data Integrity:** Blockchain's immutability ensures that stored data cannot be tampered with.
- **Confidentiality:** Encryption and access control mechanisms protect the confidentiality of data.
- **Transparency:** Blockchain provides an auditable record of data access and sharing, improving accountability.
- **Resilience:** Decentralized storage makes data more resilient to attacks and censorship.

Challenges and Considerations

- **Scalability:** Blockchain-based storage and sharing solutions can be slow and resource-intensive, which can limit their applicability in some situations.
- **Complexity:** Implementing these solutions can be complex and require specialized expertise.
- **Regulation:** The regulatory landscape surrounding blockchain and data privacy is still evolving.

Despite these challenges, blockchain offers a powerful set of tools for enhancing secure data storage and sharing. As the technology matures, we can expect to see even more innovative applications in cybersecurity and other sectors.

Identity and Access Management

- Self-sovereign identity (SSI) solutions.
- Decentralized authentication and authorization.

Identity and Access Management (IAM) with blockchain, especially when it comes to self-sovereign identity (SSI) and decentralized authentication. Let's explore this further:

The Problem with Traditional IAM

Traditional IAM systems rely on centralized authorities (like companies or governments) to store and manage our digital identities. This creates several vulnerabilities:

- **Single Point of Failure:** If the central authority is compromised, all user identities are at risk.
- **Data Breaches:** Centralized databases are attractive targets for hackers, leading to massive data breaches.
- **Lack of Control:** Users have limited control over their own data and how it is used.

How Blockchain-Based IAM Helps

Blockchain offers a decentralized and secure way to manage identities, addressing the shortcomings of traditional systems:

- **Self-Sovereign Identity (SSI):** SSI solutions, often built on blockchain, empower individuals to take control of their digital identities. Users create and manage their own identities, independent of any central authority.
- **Decentralized Authentication:** Blockchain enables decentralized authentication, where users can verify their identity without relying on a central authority. This can be done using cryptographic techniques, such as digital signatures.
- **Decentralized Authorization:** Blockchain can also be used for decentralized authorization, where access to resources is granted based on verifiable credentials and permissions stored on the blockchain.

Key Components of Blockchain-Based IAM

- **Decentralized Identifiers (DIDs):** Unique identifiers that are owned and controlled by the user.
- **Verifiable Credentials (VCs):** Digital credentials issued by trusted entities (like governments or universities) that can be verified without relying on the issuer.
- **Digital Wallets:** Secure applications where users store and manage their DIDs and VCs.

Benefits of Blockchain-Based IAM in Cybersecurity

- **Reduced Risk of Data Breaches:** Decentralized storage makes it harder for hackers to steal large amounts of identity data.
- **Improved Privacy:** Users have greater control over their data and can limit what information they share.
- **Enhanced Security:** Cryptographic techniques are used to secure and verify identities.
- **Increased Trust:** Blockchain enables trustless interactions, as users can verify credentials without relying on a central authority.
- **Interoperability:** Blockchain-based IAM can enable seamless interoperability between different systems and platforms.

Examples of Blockchain-Based IAM Applications

- **Passwordless Authentication:** Users can authenticate to websites and applications using their DID, eliminating the need for passwords.
- **Secure Data Sharing:** Individuals can securely share personal information with healthcare providers, financial institutions, or other parties without relying on intermediaries.
- **Digital Signatures:** Blockchain-based IAM can be used to create digital signatures, ensuring the authenticity and integrity of documents.
- **IoT Device Management:** Blockchain-based IAM can be used to manage the identities of IoT devices, improving their security and interoperability.

Challenges and Considerations

- **Usability:** Making blockchain-based IAM user-friendly is crucial for widespread adoption.
- **Scalability:** Blockchain-based IAM systems need to be able to handle large numbers of users and transactions.
- **Regulation:** The regulatory landscape surrounding blockchain-based IAM is still evolving.

Despite these challenges, blockchain-based IAM has the potential to revolutionize how we manage digital identities, enhancing security, privacy, and user control. By reducing our reliance on centralized authorities, blockchain-based IAM can make the internet a safer and more trustworthy place.

Threat Intelligence Sharing

Secure and efficient sharing of threat intelligence data among organizations:
the importance of threat intelligence sharing, and how blockchain can play a crucial role in making it more secure and efficient. Here's how:

The Challenge

Organizations often struggle to share threat intelligence effectively due to concerns about:

- **Data Sensitivity:** Sharing information about attacks or vulnerabilities can reveal sensitive internal details.
- **Trust:** Organizations may not fully trust other parties to handle their data responsibly.
- **Timeliness:** Sharing threat intelligence quickly is crucial, but traditional methods can be slow and cumbersome.
- **Data Integrity:** Ensuring the accuracy and authenticity of shared threat intelligence is essential.

How Blockchain Helps

Blockchain offers several advantages for enhancing threat intelligence sharing:

- **Secure and Controlled Sharing:** Blockchain enables secure data sharing with fine-grained access control. Organizations can selectively share information with trusted partners while protecting sensitive data.
- **Data Integrity and Immutability:** Blockchain's immutability ensures that shared threat intelligence cannot be tampered with, enhancing trust and reliability.
- **Transparency and Auditability:** All sharing transactions are recorded on the blockchain, creating a transparent and auditable record. This improves accountability and helps ensure data quality.
- **Decentralization:** Blockchain's decentralized nature reduces the risk of single points of failure and censorship.
- **Automation:** Smart contracts can automate the process of sharing threat intelligence, improving efficiency and timeliness.

Benefits of Blockchain-Based Threat Intelligence Sharing

- **Improved Collaboration:** Enables organizations to collaborate more effectively on threat intelligence sharing, leading to a more comprehensive view of the threat landscape.
- **Faster Response Times:** Facilitates faster sharing of threat intelligence, allowing organizations to respond more quickly to emerging threats.
- **Enhanced Data Quality:** Immutability and transparency improve the quality and reliability of shared threat intelligence.
- **Increased Trust:** Secure and controlled sharing mechanisms increase trust between participating organizations.
- **Reduced Costs:** Automation can reduce the costs associated with manual threat intelligence sharing processes.

Examples of Blockchain-Based Threat Intelligence Platforms

Several platforms are emerging that leverage blockchain for threat intelligence sharing. These platforms often provide features such as:

- Secure storage and sharing of threat indicators (IOCs).
- Automated sharing of threat intelligence based on predefined rules.
- Reputation scoring and trust mechanisms for participating organizations.
- Incentive mechanisms for sharing high-quality threat intelligence.

Challenges and Considerations

- **Scalability:** Blockchain platforms need to be able to handle large volumes of threat intelligence data.
- **Interoperability:** Ensuring interoperability between different threat intelligence platforms is crucial.
- **Standardization:** Standardized data formats and protocols are needed to facilitate seamless sharing of threat intelligence.
- **Governance:** Clear governance models are needed to manage the sharing process and ensure data quality.

Despite these challenges, blockchain has the potential to significantly improve threat intelligence sharing, enabling organizations to collaborate more effectively and stay ahead of evolving cyber threats. By leveraging the unique characteristics of blockchain, organizations can build more secure, efficient, and trustworthy threat intelligence sharing platforms.

Anti-counterfeiting and Supply Chain Security

- Tracking the origin and provenance of goods.
- Combating counterfeit products and ensuring product authenticity

You're absolutely right to focus on anti-counterfeiting and supply chain security, as these are critical areas where blockchain can make a real difference. Here's how:

The Challenge

Counterfeit products pose a significant threat to businesses and consumers alike. They can lead to financial losses, damage brand reputation, and even endanger public health and safety (think counterfeit medications or faulty parts in critical infrastructure). Traditional supply chains often lack the transparency and traceability needed to effectively combat counterfeiting.

How Blockchain Helps

Blockchain's inherent characteristics offer a powerful way to enhance supply chain security and combat counterfeiting:

- **Tracking Origin and Provenance:** Blockchain can be used to create an immutable record of a product's journey throughout the supply chain, from its origin to the end consumer. This allows for verifying the authenticity of the product and tracking its movement.
- **Unique Product Identification:** Each product can be assigned a unique identifier on the blockchain, making it easy to distinguish genuine products from counterfeits.
- **Secure Data Sharing:** Blockchain enables secure and controlled data sharing between different stakeholders in the supply chain, such as manufacturers, distributors, retailers, and consumers.
- **Transparency and Auditability:** All transactions and events related to a product are recorded on the blockchain, creating a transparent and auditable record. This makes it easier to identify and investigate instances of counterfeiting or tampering.

Applications in Cybersecurity

- **Software Supply Chain Security:** Ensuring the integrity and authenticity of software updates and dependencies is crucial for preventing malware from being introduced into systems. Blockchain can be used to track the origin and provenance of software components, ensuring that they haven't been tampered with.
- **Hardware Integrity:** Tracking hardware components throughout the supply chain can help prevent the introduction of counterfeit or compromised parts into critical systems.
- **Securing IoT Devices:** Blockchain can be used to manage the identities and data generated by IoT devices, ensuring that they are authentic and haven't been compromised. This is important for securing critical infrastructure and preventing IoT-based attacks.

Benefits of Blockchain for Anti-Counterfeiting and Supply Chain Security:

- **Increased Transparency:** Blockchain provides a transparent view of the entire supply chain, making it easier to identify and track counterfeit products.
- **Improved Traceability:** Blockchain enables end-to-end traceability of products, from origin to consumer.
- **Enhanced Trust:** Immutability and transparency build trust in the authenticity of

products.

- **Reduced Counterfeiting:** By making it harder to introduce counterfeit products into the supply chain, blockchain can help reduce counterfeiting.
- **Improved Efficiency:** Blockchain can streamline supply chain processes and reduce costs.

Challenges and Considerations:

- **Scalability:** Blockchain platforms need to be able to handle the large volumes of data generated by complex supply chains.
- **Integration:** Integrating blockchain with existing supply chain systems can be challenging.
- **Cost:** Implementing blockchain-based solutions can be expensive.
- **Regulation:** The regulatory landscape surrounding blockchain and supply chain security is still evolving.

Despite these challenges, blockchain offers a powerful set of tools for enhancing anti-counterfeiting measures and improving supply chain security. As the technology matures, we can expect to see even more innovative applications in this space, contributing to a more secure and trustworthy global marketplace

You've hit upon some of the most critical challenges and considerations facing blockchain technology, especially in its application to cybersecurity. Let's delve into each of these:

1. Scalability and Performance Limitations:
   - **The Problem:** Blockchain systems, particularly public ones, can struggle to handle high transaction volumes. The process of validating and adding transactions to the blockchain can be slow and resource-intensive, leading to bottlenecks and high transaction fees. This is a major obstacle for widespread adoption, especially in applications that require high throughput, like processing large numbers of IoT device updates or handling high-frequency financial transactions.
   - **Examples:** Bitcoin's limited transaction throughput is a well-known example of scalability challenges. As the number of Bitcoin transactions increased, transaction times and fees rose significantly.
   - **Potential Solutions:** Various scaling solutions are being developed, including:
     - **Layer-2 solutions:** These operate on top of the main blockchain, handling transactions off-chain and then periodically anchoring them to the main chain. Examples include Lightning Network and Plasma.
     - **Sharding:** This involves dividing the blockchain into smaller "shards," each of which can process transactions independently.
     - **Sidechains:** These are separate blockchains that run parallel to the main chain and can interact with it.
2. Regulatory and Legal Uncertainties:
   - **The Problem:** The regulatory landscape surrounding blockchain technology is still

evolving. There's a lack of clear legal frameworks governing the use of blockchain in many jurisdictions, creating uncertainty for businesses and hindering adoption. Issues like data privacy, cross-border transactions, and the legal status of smart contracts need clarification.

- **Examples:** The legal status of smart contracts is still being debated in many countries. Questions remain about whether smart contracts are legally binding and how they should be enforced. Data privacy regulations, like GDPR, also pose challenges for blockchain applications that involve personal data.
- **Potential Solutions:** Increased dialogue between regulators and the blockchain community is crucial to develop clear and appropriate regulations. Industry standards and best practices can also help guide businesses in navigating the regulatory landscape.

3. Security Vulnerabilities:
   - **The Problem:** While blockchain offers many security benefits, it's not immune to attacks. Several vulnerabilities can be exploited, including:
     - **Smart contract vulnerabilities:** Smart contracts, which are self-executing contracts stored on the blockchain, can contain bugs or vulnerabilities that attackers can exploit.
     - **51% attacks:** If a single entity or group gains control of more than 50% of the network's computing power, they can potentially manipulate the blockchain and double-spend cryptocurrency.
     - **Phishing and social engineering:** Users can be tricked into revealing their private keys, giving attackers access to their cryptocurrency or other assets.
     - **Key management:** Securely managing private keys is crucial, as the loss of a private key can result in the permanent loss of access to funds.
   - **Potential Solutions:** Rigorous smart contract auditing, robust consensus mechanisms, and user education are essential to mitigate these security risks. Hardware wallets and multi-signature wallets can help protect private keys.
4. Privacy Concerns:
   - **The Problem:** While some blockchains offer anonymity, the transparent nature of many blockchains can raise privacy concerns. Transactions are often publicly viewable, which can reveal sensitive information about individuals or organizations. Balancing transparency with individual privacy is a key challenge.
   - **Examples:** Tracking cryptocurrency transactions on a public blockchain can potentially reveal information about a person's financial activities.
   - **Potential Solutions:** Several privacy-enhancing techniques are being developed, including:
     - **Zero-knowledge proofs:** These allow for verifying that a statement is true without revealing any information about the statement itself.
     - **Homomorphic encryption:** This allows for performing computations on encrypted data without decrypting it.
     - **Mixing services:** These services mix cryptocurrency transactions to obscure the

origin and destination of funds.

Addressing these challenges is crucial for the long-term success of blockchain technology. Continued research, development, and collaboration between industry, academia, and regulators are essential to overcome these obstacles and unlock the full potential of blockchain for cybersecurity and other applications.

Future Directions

1. Integration of Blockchain with Other Emerging Technologies:
   - **AI and Blockchain:** Combining AI and blockchain can create intelligent and secure systems. AI can analyze blockchain data to identify patterns, detect anomalies, and predict threats. Blockchain can provide a secure and transparent platform for training and deploying AI models, ensuring data integrity and preventing manipulation.
   - **IoT and Blockchain:** Integrating blockchain with IoT can enhance the security and interoperability of IoT devices. Blockchain can be used to manage device identities, secure communication channels, and enable secure data sharing between devices. This is crucial for securing critical infrastructure and preventing IoT-based attacks.
   - **5G and Blockchain:** 5G networks offer high bandwidth and low latency, which can enable new blockchain applications, such as real-time data streaming and secure communication for IoT devices. Blockchain can also enhance the security of 5G networks themselves by providing secure authentication and authorization mechanisms.
2. Development of More Scalable and Efficient Blockchain Protocols:
   - **Addressing Scalability Challenges:** As discussed earlier, scalability is a major hurdle for blockchain adoption. Continued research and development of more scalable protocols are essential. This includes exploring Layer-2 solutions, sharding, sidechains, and other innovative approaches.
   - **Improving Efficiency:** Making blockchain systems more efficient in terms of energy consumption and transaction processing speed is crucial for reducing costs and making the technology more sustainable.
3. Addressing the Regulatory Challenges and Fostering Innovation:
   - **Clear Regulatory Frameworks:** Governments and regulatory bodies need to develop clear and consistent legal frameworks for blockchain technology. This will provide businesses with the certainty they need to invest and innovate.
   - **Balancing Innovation and Regulation:** Regulations should be designed to protect consumers and address potential risks without stifling innovation. Striking the right balance is crucial.
   - **International Collaboration:** Given the global nature of blockchain, international collaboration is essential to develop harmonized regulations and standards.
4. Raising Awareness and Education:
   - **Bridging the Knowledge Gap:** Many people are still unfamiliar with blockchain technology and its potential applications. Raising awareness and providing education

about blockchain is crucial for fostering adoption and innovation.

- **Targeted Education Programs:** Developing targeted education programs for different audiences, including developers, businesses, policymakers, and the general public, is essential.
- **Promoting Cybersecurity Best Practices:** Education should also focus on cybersecurity best practices related to blockchain, such as secure key management and smart contract development.

5. Focus on Specific Cybersecurity Applications:
   - **Strengthening Existing Solutions:** Continued development and improvement of blockchain-based solutions in areas like decentralized identity, secure data sharing, supply chain security, and threat intelligence sharing are crucial.
   - **Exploring New Applications:** Research and development should explore new and innovative ways to leverage blockchain for cybersecurity, such as using it for securing AI/ML models, building decentralized security platforms, or creating more resilient infrastructure.

By focusing on these future directions, we can unlock the full potential of blockchain technology to enhance cybersecurity and build a more secure digital world. It's a collaborative effort that requires ongoing research, innovation, and engagement from all stakeholders.

Conclusion

Blockchain technology, with its core principles of decentralization, immutability, and transparency, presents a powerful paradigm shift in how we approach cybersecurity. It offers a unique set of advantages that address some of the most pressing challenges in protecting our digital world.

Key Benefits Recap:

- **Data Integrity and Immutability:** Blockchain's inherent structure ensures that data, once recorded, cannot be altered, providing a bedrock of trust for security logs, audit trails, and sensitive records.
- **Decentralization and Resilience:** Distributing data and control across a network makes systems more resistant to single points of failure and attacks.
- **Enhanced Identity and Access Management:** Blockchain empowers individuals with self-sovereign identity, reducing reliance on vulnerable centralized systems and giving users greater control over their data.
- **Secure Data Sharing and Collaboration:** Blockchain enables secure and auditable data sharing between organizations, fostering collaboration on threat intelligence and other security-related tasks.
- **Improved Supply Chain Security:** Tracking goods and materials on a blockchain enhances transparency and helps prevent counterfeiting, ensuring the integrity of products and components.

- **Increased Trust and Transparency:** Blockchain fosters trust in digital interactions by providing a shared, verifiable record of transactions and events.

Revolutionizing the Cybersecurity Landscape:
Blockchain has the potential to revolutionize cybersecurity by:

- **Shifting from Reactive to Proactive Security:** By enabling secure data sharing and collaboration, blockchain can help organizations anticipate and prevent attacks before they occur.
- **Strengthening Trust and Accountability:** Blockchain's transparency and immutability enhance trust in digital systems and improve accountability for security-related decisions.
- **Empowering Individuals:** Self-sovereign identity solutions give individuals greater control over their digital identities and protect their privacy.
- **Securing the Future of the Digital Economy:** As our world becomes increasingly interconnected, blockchain can play a crucial role in securing the digital infrastructure that underpins our economy and society.

The Path Forward:
While blockchain offers immense promise, realizing its full potential in cybersecurity requires continued effort. Further research and development are essential to:

- **Address Scalability and Performance Limitations:** Overcoming the scalability challenges of blockchain is crucial for its widespread adoption.
- **Enhance Security and Privacy:** Continued research is needed to identify and mitigate potential vulnerabilities in blockchain systems and to develop stronger privacy-preserving techniques.
- **Navigate the Regulatory Landscape:** Clear and consistent regulatory frameworks are needed to provide businesses with the certainty they need to invest in blockchain-based solutions.
- **Foster Collaboration and Innovation:** Collaboration between researchers, developers, businesses, and policymakers is essential to drive innovation and accelerate the adoption of blockchain in cybersecurity.

Blockchain technology is not a silver bullet, but it is a powerful tool that can significantly enhance our ability to protect against cyber threats. By embracing its potential and addressing its challenges, we can build a more secure and resilient digital future.

4

Quantum Computing and Its Impact on Cybersecurity

The advent of quantum computing signifies a revolutionary shift in computational science, reshaping how information is processed and secured. Unlike classical computing, which relies on binary bits (0s and 1s), quantum computing uses the principles of quantum mechanics to exploit quantum bits, or qubits. These qubits exhibit unique properties such as superposition, allowing them to exist in multiple states simultaneously, and entanglement, wherein qubits become interconnected regardless of the distance between them. These capabilities enable quantum computers to execute parallel computations on an unprecedented scale, making them exponentially more powerful than their classical counterparts for certain types of problems. The historical foundations of quantum computing can be traced back to the early twentieth century with the development of quantum mechanics. In the 1980s, scientists such as Richard Feynman and David Deutsch envisioned the application of quantum principles to computation, leading to the formulation of quantum algorithms. Since then, research in quantum computing has rapidly advanced, featuring significant milestones such as Shor's algorithm in 1994, which illustrated that quantum computers can efficiently factor large numbers, a direct challenge to contemporary encryption methods. Similarly, Grover's algorithm, introduced in 1996, demonstrated a quantum speedup for search-related problems, thereby underscoring the potential for quantum computing to surpass classical systems in data retrieval and optimisation tasks. As the field continues to advance, quantum computing presents a dual-faceted influence on cybersecurity. On one hand, its substantial computational power threatens to break widely used encryption techniques, challenging the security of sensitive digital communications, blockchain systems, and confidential transactions. On the other hand, it also provides opportunities for enhancing cybersecurity through quantum cryptographic techniques, advanced threat detection systems, and the optimisation of security protocols.

This chapter provides a comprehensive exploration of the fundamental principles of quantum computing, its historical development, and its implications for cybersecurity. It examines the risks that quantum computing to existing cryptographic systems, discusses proactive measures to mitigate these threats, and explores the potential benefits that quantum computing may bring to the field of cybersecurity. By understanding these aspects, organisations and individuals can better prepare for the emerging quantum era and navigate the complex transition towards quantum-safe security solutions.

A Brief History of Quantum Computing

Quantum computing is based on the fundamental principles of quantum mechanics, which emerged in the early 20th century as researchers sought to understand the behaviour of subatomic particles. Theoretical advancements in quantum mechanics led to a novel understanding of concepts such as superposition and entanglement, thereby establishing the foundation for their application in computing. However, it was not until the 1980s that the idea of quantum computation received substantial attention.

In 1981, physicist Richard Feynman posited that classical computers exhibited inefficiencies when tasked with simulating quantum systems, proposing that quantum computers could serve as a more effective alternative. This idea ignited further research into quantum computational models. In 1994, mathematician Peter Shor illustrated the potential of quantum computing by developing an algorithm capable of factoring large numbers exponentially faster than classical methods, presenting a serious threat to widely used encryption techniques. In 1996, Lov Grover introduced an algorithm that significantly expedited search operations in unsorted databases, showcasing yet another practical advantage of quantum computing.

Since the early 2000s, research in the field of quantum computing has shifted from purely theoretical work to experimental implementations. Leading technology firms such as IBM, Google, and D-Wave have invested heavily in advancing quantum processors, aiming for the realisation of stable and scalable quantum systems. A significant milestone was achieved in 2019 when Google publicly declared its claim of "quantum supremacy," demonstrating that a quantum computer could solve a problem unattainable by even the most sophisticated classical supercomputers. As research and technological advancements progress, emphasis is now placed on addressing significant challenges, including quantum error correction, qubit stability, and scalability. Researchers aim to harness the full potential of quantum computing to revolutionise various industries, particularly in the domain of cybersecurity, where it has the capacity to both disrupt and enhance encryption methodologies. The field continues to evolve, promising substantial breakthroughs in computational power, optimisation, and secure communications. As research progresses, scientists aim to develop stable and scalable quantum systems that will unlock the full potential of quantum computing across industries, including cybersecurity.

Basics of Quantum Computing

Quantum computing represents a significant advancement over classical computing through the application of quantum mechanics. In contrast to classical computers, which operate using bits (0 or 1), quantum computers employ qubits, capable of existing in multiple states simultaneously due to the phenomenon of superposition. This property enables them to explore numerous solutions concurrently, thereby considerably enhancing efficiency. Furthermore, a critical element of quantum computing is entanglement, whereby qubits become interconnected such that the state of one qubit influences the state of another, irrespective of the distance separating them, thereby facilitating unique computational capabilities. Additionally, quantum tunneling allows particles to bypass energy barriers, leading to more efficient problem-solving in fields like optimization and materials science.
Superposition: In classical computing, a bit can exist in one of two states—either 0 or 1. However, quantum computing introduces the concept of superposition, whereby a quantum bit (qubit) can exist in both states simultaneously. This enables a quantum computer to process multiple computations at once, significantly enhancing its computational power. Rather than solving problems sequentially as classical computers do, quantum computers explore numerous possibilities in parallel, rendering them exponentially faster for certain types of problems, such as cryptographic analysis and complex simulations.

Entanglement: Another fundamental quantum property is entanglement, which describes a unique correlation between two or more qubits. When qubits become entangled, the state of one qubit is instantaneously connected to the state of another, regardless of the distance between them. This property is essential for quantum communication and quantum computing, as it facilitates quicker data transfer and more efficient problem-solving techniques that classical systems cannot replicate. Entanglement is also the foundation of quantum networking and is crucial for secure quantum cryptography.

Quantum Tunnelling: In classical physics, a particle requires sufficient energy to overcome a barrier. However, quantum mechanics allows particles to traverse these barriers through quantum tunnelling. This principle allows quantum computers to uncover solutions to problems that involve navigating intricate landscapes, such as optimisation problems in logistics, finance, and artificial intelligence. By 'tunnelling' through potential solutions rather than evaluating each one sequentially, quantum computers can achieve optimal answers much faster than classical systems.

Together, these principles of superposition, entanglement, and quantum tunnelling constitute the foundational elements of quantum computing. These principles empower quantum computers to solve problems that are virtually impossible for classical computers, opening the way for revolutionary advancements in cybersecurity, artificial intelligence, and data science. As research and development continue to progress, a comprehensive understanding of these fundamental concepts will be crucial to harnessing the full potential of quantum computing in practical applications.

Why Quantum Computing Matters

Quantum computing has significant implications across various fields, particularly in addressing computational problems practically infeasible for classical computers. Its applications encompass:

- **Cybersecurity:** Quantum computing presents significant risks and opportunities for modern digital security. On one hand, its computational power threatens current encryption methods, such as RSA and ECC, which rely on the infeasibility of factoring large numbers. Algorithms like Shor's can break these encryptions in polynomial time, rendering traditional cryptographic systems obsolete. On the other hand, quantum computing also introduces innovative security solutions, such as Quantum Key Distribution (QKD), which leverages the principles of quantum mechanics to establish theoretically unbreakable encryption by detecting eavesdropping attempts. Additionally, post-quantum cryptography (PQC) is being developed to provide quantum-resistant encryption techniques, ensuring secure communication in a future where quantum computers exist.
- **Artificial Intelligence & Machine Learning:** Quantum computing is set to revolutionise artificial intelligence (AI) and machine learning (ML) by significantly enhancing the efficiency and speed of data processing, model training, and optimisation. Unlike classical computing, which processes data either sequentially or in parallel within limited parameters, quantum computing utilises superposition and entanglement to execute complex computations simultaneously across multiple states.

Quantum-enhanced machine learning (QML) efficiently processes high-dimensional data using quantum algorithms such as Quantum Support Vector Machines (QSVM), Quantum Boltzmann Machines, and Variational Quantum Circuits. These quantum models can accelerate the identification of patterns, reduce computational complexity, and optimise hyperparameter tuning for deep learning models. Furthermore, research indicates that quantum computers can significantly enhance natural language processing (NLP), generative AI, and reinforcement learning by addressing combinatorial and probabilistic problems more efficiently than classical systems. This breakthrough carries substantial implications for cybersecurity, where quantum AI can improve anomaly detection, automate threat prediction, and optimise cryptographic defences in real-time. Though practical implementations of QML remain in early development, companies such as Google, IBM, and Microsoft are actively exploring its potential to transform industries that rely on advanced data analytics and decision-making systems.

Optimization Problems: Quantum computing offers a transformative method for addressing complex optimisation challenges that are computationally intensive for classical systems.

Fields such as logistics, supply chain management, financial modelling, and operations research stand to gain significantly from quantum-enhanced optimisation techniques. Quantum algorithms, such as the Quantum Approximate Optimisation Algorithm (QAOA) and Variational Quantum Eigensolver (VQE), allow businesses to discover optimal solutions to problems involving multiple variables with interdependent constraints. These problems often require evaluating an exponential number of possible configurations, which classical computers struggle with due to time and resource limitations.

For example, in logistics and supply chain management, quantum computing can optimize delivery routes, inventory management, and warehouse operations by processing real-time data with unprecedented efficiency. In financial modelling, quantum techniques enable more accurate risk assessments, portfolio optimisations, and fraud detection mechanisms by analysing vast datasets in parallel. As research and development in quantum computing continue, its applications in optimization problems will likely redefine efficiency and decision-making across industries, paving the way for a more robust, data-driven future.

Scientific Research: Quantum computing plays a pivotal role in advancing scientific research by enabling highly accurate simulations that were previously infeasible for classical computers. One of its most promising applications is in understanding chemical reactions at the quantum level, allowing researchers to model complex molecular interactions with unprecedented precision. This capability has profound implications for pharmaceutical research, where quantum simulations can accelerate drug discovery by predicting how molecules interact, reducing the need for costly and time-consuming experimental trials.

In addition to pharmaceuticals, quantum computing is revolutionising materials science by enabling the development of novel materials with improved properties. Researchers can simulate the behaviour of new alloys, superconductors, and nanomaterials, optimising them for various applications, including energy storage and advanced computing hardware.

Furthermore, quantum computing is transforming fields such as climate modelling and genomics. Climate scientists employ quantum algorithms to analyse vast datasets related to atmospheric changes, enhancing predictive models for extreme weather events. In genomics, quantum-powered algorithms facilitate the analysis of complex genetic data, potentially unlocking new methods for personalised medicine and the treatment of genetic disorders.
Although these advancements are currently in the early stages, ongoing research and development conducted by institutions such as MIT, Google, and IBM are extending the limits of what quantum computing can accomplish in scientific discovery. As quantum hardware continues to evolve, its impact on research and innovation will expand, clearing the way for transformative breakthroughs across various.

Quantum Threats to Cryptography

Modern cryptographic systems are predicated on the assumption that certain mathematical problems, such as integer factorisation and discrete logarithms, are computationally infeasible for classical computers to resolve within a reasonable timeframe. The security of prevalent encryption schemes, including RSA and elliptic curve cryptography (ECC), relies on this complexity. However, the emergence of quantum computing fundamentally challenges this security model by introducing quantum algorithms capable of solving these problems exponentially faster than classical algorithms. This shift threatens to undermine the foundations of modern cryptographic protocols, making encrypted data vulnerable to decryption once large-scale quantum computers become practical. Key threats posed by quantum computing include:

- **Shor's Algorithm and Public-Key Cryptography:** Public-key cryptography, including RSA and Elliptic Curve Cryptography (ECC), relies on the computational difficulty of factoring large prime numbers or solving discrete logarithm problems. These encryption methods are widely used to secure online transactions, digital signatures, and confidential communications.
- **Grover's Algorithm and Symmetric Cryptography:** Grover's algorithm reduces brute-force search times, weakening encryption schemes like AES unless key lengths are significantly increased.
- **Threats to Blockchain:** Blockchain security depends on cryptographic hash functions and public-key cryptography, both of which quantum computing could potentially break, leading to risks for cryptocurrencies and decentralised applications.
- **Quantum Malware and Network Attacks:** Quantum-enhanced malware and quantum-based attacks could exploit vulnerabilities in classical and emerging quantum communication networks.

Preparing for a Post-Quantum World

The rapid advancement of quantum computing necessitates a proactive approach to safeguarding cybersecurity and ensuring data integrity in a post-quantum world. As widely used cryptographic algorithms like RSA, ECC, and Diffie-Hellman key exchange are vulnerable to quantum attacks, organisations, governments, and technology leaders must immediately transition towards quantum-resistant solutions. Preparing for this transition demands a comprehensive approach, integrating new cryptographic standards, infrastructure upgrades, and policy adaptations.

- **Development of Post-Quantum Cryptography (PQC):** The National Institute of Standards and Technology (NIST) has led efforts to standardise quantum-resistant cryptographic algorithms. Post-quantum cryptography (PQC) development focuses on creating encryption methods that remain secure against quantum threats while being deployable on existing digital infrastructure. Techniques such as lattice-based cryptography, hash-based signatures, code-based cryptography, and multivariate polynomial cryptography have emerged as promising candidates. For instance, lattice-based cryptography utilises mathematical problems that even quantum computers find difficult to solve efficiently, making it one of the most promising quantum-resistant cryptographic solutions.

- **Quantum Key Distribution (QKD) and Secure Communication:** Quantum Key Distribution (QKD) is a groundbreaking advancement in secure communications. It utilizes the principles of quantum mechanics to establish highly secure encryption keys. Protocols such as BB84 and E91 guarantee that any attempts at eavesdropping disturb the quantum state, immediately alerting the communicating parties of potential security breaches. While QKD presents a promising outlook for quantum-secure communication, it requires significant investment in quantum network infrastructure, including fiber-optic and satellite-based transmission systems.
- **Hybrid Cryptographic Systems:** As organisations transition towards a quantum-safe ecosystem, hybrid cryptographic models that combine classical and post-quantum cryptographic algorithms provide an interim solution. These hybrid systems ensure resilience by remaining compatible with existing security infrastructures while integrating quantum-resistant techniques to mitigate potential vulnerabilities.
- **Upgrading Cryptographic Infrastructure:** Organizations must comprehensively assess their cryptographic assets to determine their vulnerability to quantum attacks. This includes:
    - Identifying and cataloguing existing cryptographic implementations across networks, applications, and databases.
    - Evaluating the quantum susceptibility of encryption protocols currently in use.
    - Developing a structured migration roadmap for transitioning to post-quantum cryptographic solutions.
    - Ensuring compliance with emerging quantum security regulations and standards.
- **Quantum-Resistant Blockchain and Digital Ledger Technologies:** Blockchain technology fundamentally relies on cryptographic hash functions and digital signatures to ensure security and maintain data integrity. However, advancements in quantum computing have the potential to compromise these cryptographic constructs, thereby jeopardising blockchain-based applications such as cryptocurrencies, digital contracts, and decentralised finance. As a result, researchers are actively exploring quantum-resistant blockchain solutions, including the integration of lattice-based cryptography and quantum-safe digital signature schemes to enhance blockchain security.
- **Investment in Quantum-Safe Security Research and Workforce Development:** The transition to a post-quantum security landscape requires investment in quantum computing research, workforce development, and cybersecurity training.

Organisations must train their cybersecurity teams on quantum threats and quantum-resistant cryptographic techniques. Collaboration among governments, academia, and private sector entities is essential for cultivating a skilled workforce capable of navigating the quantum transition.

- **Global Policy and Regulatory Adaptation:** As quantum computing develops, governments and regulatory bodies must create frameworks for quantum cybersecurity standards, risk assessment models, and compliance mandates. International cooperation will be essential in setting security benchmarks for quantum-safe communications, digital transactions, and national security infrastructure.

By proactively adopting these strategies, organisations can mitigate the risks associated with quantum computing while embracing its transformative benefits. The transition to a post-quantum world necessitates foresight, collaboration, and ongoing innovation to safeguard digital security in the face of rapidly advancing computational capabilities.

Opportunities Presented by Quantum Computing

While quantum computing presents significant security challenges, it also presents groundbreaking opportunities across various fields, including cybersecurity, artificial intelligence, optimisation, and scientific research. Harnessing the power of quantum mechanics enables faster computations, more efficient problem-solving, and advancements in secure communication. Below are the key areas where quantum computing is expected to drive innovation:

- **Quantum Cryptography and Secure Communication:** Quantum cryptography, particularly Quantum Key Distribution (QKD), guarantees secure communication by utilising the principles of quantum mechanics. Unlike traditional encryption, QKD identifies any eavesdropping attempts by detecting disturbances in quantum states. This positions QKD as a promising solution for military, financial, and governmental communications. Furthermore, researchers are developing post-quantum cryptographic (PQC) algorithms, including lattice-based and hash-based cryptography, to establish encryption methods that are robust against quantum attacks.
- **Enhanced Threat Detection and Cybersecurity AI:** Quantum computing has the potential to transform threat detection by processing vast quantities of cybersecurity data in real time. Quantum-enhanced machine learning algorithms, such as Quantum Neural Networks (QNN) and Quantum Support Vector Machines (QSVM), can detect patterns and anomalies in large datasets more efficiently than classical methods. This advancement will enhance cybersecurity monitoring, intrusion detection systems, and real-time threat intelligence.
- **Optimisation of Security Protocols and Authentication Systems:** Quantum

algorithms enhance the efficiency of security protocols by improving authentication mechanisms, digital signatures, and cryptographic key management. Techniques such as quantum-enhanced random number generation (QRNG) deliver stronger cryptographic keys, rendering authentication systems more resilient against cyber threats.

- **Advancements in AI and Machine Learning**: Quantum computing accelerates the development of AI models, enabling more sophisticated data analysis, optimisation, and decision-making. Quantum algorithms, such as Quantum Boltzmann Machines and Variational Quantum Circuits, facilitate more rapid training of machine learning models. These advancements will influence AI-driven applications, including natural language processing (NLP), image recognition, and fraud detection.
- **Scientific Research and Drug Discovery:** Quantum computing enhances scientific simulations by accurately modelling chemical reactions, molecular interactions, and material properties. In pharmaceuticals, quantum simulations help researchers in developing new drugs by predicting molecular behaviour with high precision, thereby reducing the time required for drug discovery. Similarly, quantum-enabled materials science can lead to the development of advanced materials for secure computing hardware.
- **Financial Risk Assessment and Fraud Detection:** Quantum algorithms enhance the optimisation of financial risk modelling by effectively analysing vast datasets. Banking institutions and economic organisations can utilise quantum computing for fraud detection, portfolio optimisation, and high-frequency trading. By recognising patterns within transactional data, quantum-enhanced fraud detection systems can prevent fraudulent activities in real time.
- **Supply Chain and Logistics Optimisation:** Industries such as transportation and manufacturing depend on intricate logistical systems that necessitate efficient resource allocation. Quantum computing offers advanced optimisation techniques, enhancing global supply chain management by reducing costs and maximising efficiency. Quantum-enhanced route optimisation can significantly benefit the aviation, shipping, and e-commerce sectors.

Conclusion

Quantum computing represents both a formidable challenge and a transformative opportunity for cybersecurity. Its ability to break classical cryptographic systems necessitates a shift toward quantum-safe security measures. By adopting post-quantum cryptographic solutions, investing in quantum-resistant infrastructure, and leveraging quantum computing's advantages for threat detection and optimisation, organisations can secure their digital assets in the quantum era. The transition to a post-quantum world requires strategic foresight, collaboration, and continuous innovation to safeguard cybersecurity in the face of revolutionary computational advancements.

5

Cloud Security Challenges and Solutions

As a Silicon Valley tech expert in the early years of Web 2.0, I have witnessed some interesting developments in the Cloud architecture community and how "Cloud computing" and "Cybersecurity" interact towards building a concept called "Cloud security".

Thus, in this chapter I am building a conversation on one and half decades of study into one chapter, on how we can improvise the cloud security landscape - build on a robust architecture for the future and make our cloud infrastructure impregnable to security attacks for a safe and secure online space keeping data privacy and data security as our forerunners in this discussion.

Let's dive into the complex world of cloud security challenges and their corresponding solutions. Cloud computing offers incredible benefits, but it also introduces unique security risks that require careful consideration.

Introduction: The Cloud Security Landscape

The rapid adoption of cloud computing has revolutionized how businesses operate, offering scalability, flexibility, and cost-effectiveness. However, this shift also presents a new set of security challenges. Traditional on-premises security models often don't translate directly to the cloud, and organizations must adapt their strategies to protect data and applications in this shared and dynamic environment. This discussion will explore the key security challenges organizations face in the cloud and examine the solutions available to mitigate these risks. It's crucial to understand that cloud security is a shared responsibility - the cloud provider is responsible for securing the *underlying infrastructure*, while the customer is responsible for securing the *data and applications* they deploy in the cloud. This "shared responsibility model" is fundamental to cloud security.

Let's define cloud computing and its various forms, along with its benefits and growing importance in the context of cybersecurity.

Defining Cloud Computing

Cloud computing is the on-demand delivery of IT resources—everything from applications to data centers—over the Internet. Instead of owning and maintaining physical data centers and servers, you can access technology services, as you need them, from a cloud provider.

Different Types of Cloud Computing

Cloud computing is typically categorized into three main service models:

- **Infrastructure as a Service (IaaS):** Provides access to computing resources like virtual machines, storage, and networks. You manage the operating system, applications, and data. Think of it like renting the raw materials and tools to build your IT infrastructure. Examples include Amazon EC2, Microsoft Azure Virtual Machines, and Google Compute Engine.
- **Platform as a Service (PaaS):** Offers a platform for developing, running, and managing applications without managing the underlying infrastructure. You focus on your code; the provider handles the servers, operating systems, and other infrastructure components. Examples include AWS Elastic Beanstalk, Google App Engine, and Heroku.
- **Software as a Service (SaaS):** Delivers software applications over the Internet, on demand. You access the software through a web browser or app; the provider manages the application and its underlying infrastructure. Examples include Salesforce, Google Workspace, and Microsoft 365.

Benefits of Cloud Computing

- **Scalability:** Easily scale resources up or down based on demand, ensuring you have the necessary capacity without overspending.
- **Flexibility:** Access resources from anywhere with an internet connection, enabling remote work and greater agility.
- **Cost-Effectiveness:** Reduce capital expenditures on hardware and software, and pay only for the resources you use.
- **Increased Agility:** Deploy applications and services quickly, accelerating time to market.
- **Improved Collaboration:** Cloud-based tools facilitate collaboration among teams, regardless of location.
- **Disaster Recovery:** Cloud services can provide robust disaster recovery capabilities, ensuring business continuity.

The Growing Reliance on Cloud Services in Reference to Cybersecurity

The increasing reliance on cloud services has profound implications for cybersecurity. As organizations migrate their data and applications to the cloud, they become subject to a new set of security challenges. Traditional security perimeters disappear, and organizations must adapt their security strategies to protect data and applications in a shared and dynamic cloud environment. This requires a shift in mindset, focusing on:

- **Shared Responsibility:** Understanding the shared responsibility model between the cloud provider and the customer.
- **Data Security:** Implementing robust data encryption, access control, and data loss prevention measures.
- **Identity and Access Management:** Securing user accounts and managing access to cloud resources.
- **Network Security:** Protecting cloud networks from unauthorized access and attacks.
- **Compliance:** Meeting regulatory requirements for data privacy and security.

In essence, cloud computing offers tremendous opportunities, but its widespread adoption necessitates a strong focus on cybersecurity to mitigate the inherent risks and ensure the safety and integrity of data and applications in the cloud.

The Unique Security Challenges of the Cloud

Some of the most pressing security challenges that organizations face when migrating to the cloud. Let's examine each of these in detail:

- **Shared Responsibility Model:** This is *the* foundational concept in cloud security. It dictates that security is a joint effort between the cloud provider and the customer. The provider is responsible for securing the *infrastructure*(physical data centers, hardware, networking), while the customer is responsible for securing the *data and applications* they deploy *on* that infrastructure. Misunderstanding this model can lead to significant security gaps. Customers often mistakenly assume the provider handles everything, leaving their own data and applications vulnerable.
- **Data Breaches and Data Loss:** Data breaches are a major concern in the cloud. They can occur due to various reasons, including misconfigurations, vulnerabilities in applications, compromised accounts, or malicious attacks. Data loss, on the other hand, can result from accidental deletion, hardware failure (less common with reputable providers but still possible), or ransomware attacks. The distributed nature of cloud data can make it challenging to track and manage, increasing the risk of breaches and loss.
- **Account Hijacking and Unauthorized Access:** Cloud environments rely heavily on user accounts and credentials. Account hijacking, often through phishing or weak passwords, can give attackers access to sensitive data and systems. Unauthorized access can also occur due to misconfigured permissions or vulnerabilities in access control mechanisms. The ease of provisioning and accessing cloud resources can also

inadvertently broaden the attack surface.

- **Insider Threats and Malicious Activity:** Insider threats, whether intentional or accidental, pose a significant risk in the cloud. Employees with privileged access can potentially misuse their access to steal data or sabotage systems. Malicious activity can also originate from compromised accounts or third-party vendors. The cloud's collaborative nature can sometimes blur the lines of access and control, making insider threats more difficult to detect.
- **Compliance and Regulatory Requirements:** Organizations in regulated industries (healthcare, finance, government) must comply with strict data privacy and security regulations (HIPAA, PCI DSS, GDPR, etc.). Migrating to the cloud can complicate compliance efforts, as organizations must ensure that their cloud deployments meet these requirements. Data residency, data sovereignty, and auditability are key considerations in cloud compliance.

Key Considerations Related to These Challenges

- **Visibility and Control:** Maintaining visibility and control over data and applications in the cloud can be challenging, especially in multi-cloud or hybrid cloud environments.
- **Complexity:** Cloud environments can be complex, making it difficult to understand and manage security risks.
- **Skills Gap:** There's a shortage of skilled cloud security professionals, making it difficult for organizations to implement and manage effective cloud security programs.
- **Evolving Threat Landscape:** The cloud threat landscape is constantly evolving, requiring organizations to stay up-to-date on the latest threats and vulnerabilities.

Addressing these challenges requires a comprehensive cloud security strategy that includes robust security controls, continuous monitoring, and a strong understanding of the shared responsibility model.

Key Cloud Security Challenges

1. Data Breaches
   - **The Challenge:** Cloud environments often store vast amounts of sensitive data, making them a prime target for attackers. Data breaches can result from various vulnerabilities, including misconfigurations, weak access controls, and application vulnerabilities.
   - **Why it's Critical:** Data breaches can lead to financial losses, reputational damage, legal liabilities, and loss of customer trust.
   - **Example:** A misconfigured cloud storage bucket exposes sensitive customer data to the public internet, leading to a massive data breach.
2. Misconfigurations
   - **The Challenge:** Cloud environments offer a wide range of configuration options, and misconfigurations are common. These misconfigurations can leave systems exposed to

unauthorized access and attacks.
- **Why it's Critical:** Misconfigurations can create significant security vulnerabilities that attackers can easily exploit.
- **Example:** A security group in a cloud environment is misconfigured to allow inbound traffic from any IP address, exposing the underlying systems to potential attacks.

3. Inadequate Identity and Access Management (IAM)
   - **The Challenge:** Cloud environments rely heavily on user accounts and credentials, and managing access to cloud resources can be complex. Inadequate IAM practices, such as weak passwords or excessive permissions, can lead to unauthorized access and account hijacking.
   - **Why it's Critical:** IAM is the foundation of cloud security. Weak IAM practices can undermine all other security efforts.
   - **Example:** An employee uses a weak password for their cloud account, which is then compromised by an attacker, giving them access to sensitive data and systems.
4. Insecure Interfaces and APIs
   - **The Challenge:** Cloud services often rely on APIs for communication and integration. Insecure APIs can be exploited by attackers to gain unauthorized access to cloud resources or to steal data.
   - **Why it's Critical:** APIs are a critical attack surface in cloud environments. Securing APIs is essential for protecting cloud resources.
   - **Example:** An API used by a mobile application to access cloud data is vulnerable to injection attacks, allowing attackers to manipulate the API and gain access to unauthorized data.
5. Insider Threats
   - **The Challenge:** Insider threats, whether intentional or accidental, pose a significant risk in cloud environments. Employees with privileged access can potentially misuse their access to steal data or sabotage systems.
   - **Why it's Critical:** Insider threats can be difficult to detect and can cause significant damage.
   - **Example:** A disgruntled employee with access to sensitive data downloads the data to a personal device and then leaves the company, potentially exposing the data to unauthorized parties.
6. Lack of Visibility
   - **The Challenge:** Maintaining visibility into cloud environments can be challenging, especially in multi-cloud or hybrid cloud deployments. Lack of visibility can make it difficult to detect and respond to security incidents.
   - **Why it's Critical:** Without adequate visibility, organizations may be unaware of security threats or vulnerabilities in their cloud environments.
   - **Example:** An organization uses multiple cloud providers, and it lacks a centralized view of its security posture across all cloud environments, making it difficult to identify and manage security risks.
7. Compliance Challenges

- **The Challenge:** Organizations in regulated industries must comply with various data privacy and security regulations. Migrating to the cloud can complicate compliance efforts, as organizations must ensure that their cloud deployments meet these requirements.
- **Why it's Critical:** Failure to comply with regulations can lead to fines, legal penalties, and reputational damage.
- **Example:** A healthcare organization stores patient medical records in the cloud, and it must ensure that its cloud environment complies with HIPAA regulations regarding the privacy and security of protected health information.

These are just some of the key cloud security challenges that organizations face. Addressing these challenges requires a comprehensive cloud security strategy that includes robust security controls, continuous monitoring, and a strong understanding of the shared responsibility model.

Data Security:

- Data Breaches in Transit and at Rest:
  - **In Transit:** Data moving between systems (e.g., from a user's browser to a cloud server) is vulnerable to interception. Attackers can use techniques like "man-in-the-middle" attacks to steal or modify data.
  - **At Rest:** Data stored in cloud storage (databases, object storage, etc.) is susceptible to unauthorized access. Breaches can occur due to misconfigurations, compromised credentials, or vulnerabilities in storage systems.
- Protecting Sensitive Data (PII, PHI, Financial Data):
  - **PII (Personally Identifiable Information):** Data that can identify an individual (name, address, social security number, etc.).
  - **PHI (Protected Health Information):** Medical records and other health-related data.
  - **Financial Data:** Credit card numbers, bank account details, transaction history. Protecting this data is paramount due to strict regulations and the high value to attackers.
- Ensuring Data Privacy and Compliance (GDPR, CCPA):
  - **GDPR (General Data Protection Regulation):** A European Union regulation that sets strict requirements for data privacy and security. It applies to any organization that collects or processes the personal data of EU residents, regardless of where the organization is located.
  - **CCPA (California Consumer Privacy Act):** A California law that grants consumers greater control over their personal data. It has influenced other US states to adopt similar legislation. Both GDPR and CCPA emphasize data minimization, purpose limitation, and data subject rights.

Key Data Security Practices:

- **Encryption:** Encrypt data both in transit (using TLS/SSL) and at rest (using encryption at the storage level).
- **Access Control:** Implement strong access control mechanisms (role-based access control, multi-factor authentication) to limit who can access sensitive data.
- **Data Loss Prevention (DLP):** Use DLP tools to prevent sensitive data from leaving the organization's control.
- **Regular Audits:** Conduct regular security audits to identify vulnerabilities and ensure compliance with regulations.
- **Data Masking and Tokenization:** These techniques can be used to protect sensitive data while still allowing it to be used for testing or development purposes.
- **Data Residency and Sovereignty:** Understand where your data is physically stored and ensure that it complies with relevant data residency and sovereignty regulations.

Account Hijacking and Unauthorized Access:
These are closely related and represent significant threats in cloud environments:

- **Account Hijacking:** Occurs when an attacker gains control of a legitimate user account. This is often achieved through phishing, malware, or credential stuffing (using stolen credentials from other breaches).
- **Unauthorized Access:** Refers to any access to systems or data by an individual who does not have legitimate permission. This can be due to account hijacking, misconfigured permissions, or exploiting vulnerabilities in access control systems.

Key Security Practices to Prevent Account Hijacking and Unauthorized Access:

- **Multi-Factor Authentication (MFA):** Require users to provide multiple forms of authentication (password, code from a mobile app, biometric scan) to verify their identity. This makes it significantly harder for attackers to gain access even if they have stolen a password.
- **Strong Passwords:** Enforce strong password policies (minimum length, complexity, regular changes).
- **Principle of Least Privilege:** Grant users only the minimum necessary permissions to perform their job functions.
- **Regular Security Awareness Training:** Educate users about phishing scams, social engineering tactics, and other threats that can lead to account hijacking.
- **Monitor for Suspicious Activity:** Use security tools to monitor user activity and identify suspicious login attempts or other anomalous behavior.
- **Regularly Review Permissions:** Periodically review user permissions to ensure they are still appropriate and revoke access for former employees or users who no longer need it.
- **Implement Zero Trust Security:** This model assumes no implicit trust and requires verification for every access request, regardless of whether the user is inside or outside the network.

By implementing these data security and access control practices, organizations can significantly reduce the risk of data breaches and unauthorized access in the cloud. A layered security approach, combining technical controls with user education and strong security policies, is essential for protecting sensitive data and maintaining a secure cloud environment.

Account Hijacking and Unauthorized Access: A Deeper Dive

These two concepts are intertwined. Account hijacking is often a *means* to gain unauthorized access.

- **Account Hijacking:** This occurs when an attacker gains control of a legitimate user account. Common methods include:
    - **Phishing:** Deceptive emails or websites trick users into revealing their credentials.
    - **Malware:** Malicious software steals credentials from infected devices.
    - **Credential Stuffing:** Attackers use lists of stolen credentials (from other breaches) to try and gain access to cloud accounts.
    - **Brute-Force Attacks:** Repeatedly trying different password combinations until the correct one is found (less effective with strong passwords and account lockout policies).
- **Unauthorized Access:** This encompasses any access to systems or data by an individual (or process) without legitimate permission. It can be a *result* of account hijacking, but it can also occur through other means:
    - **Misconfigured Permissions:** Overly permissive access controls allow users to access resources they shouldn't.
    - **Exploiting Vulnerabilities:** Attackers can exploit software vulnerabilities to bypass access controls and gain unauthorized access.
    - **Insider Threats:** Malicious or negligent insiders can abuse their legitimate access for unauthorized purposes.

Specific Threats in Cloud Environments:

- **Weak Passwords and Compromised Credentials:** Cloud accounts are particularly vulnerable to weak or compromised credentials. The ease of accessing cloud resources from anywhere makes these accounts a prime target for attackers. Cloud services often provide APIs for management, and if these APIs are secured with weak credentials, they become an easy entry point.
- **Insider Threats and Privilege Abuse:** Insider threats are a significant concern in the cloud. Employees with privileged access (e.g., administrators) can potentially misuse their access to steal data, sabotage systems, or grant unauthorized access to others. The cloud's collaborative nature can sometimes blur the lines of access, making it harder to monitor and control insider activity.
- **Lateral Movement within the Cloud Environment:** Once an attacker has

compromised an account, they can use that access to move laterally within the cloud environment. This means they can jump from one system to another, escalating their privileges and gaining access to more sensitive data and resources. The interconnected nature of cloud environments can make lateral movement easier if proper security measures are not in place. For example, if an attacker gains access to a development server, and that server has access to a production database due to misconfigured IAM roles, the attacker can then pivot to the production database.

Key Security Practices to Mitigate These Threats:

- **Multi-Factor Authentication (MFA):** This is *essential* for all cloud accounts, especially privileged accounts.
- **Strong Password Policies:** Enforce complexity requirements, minimum length, and regular password changes.
- **Principle of Least Privilege:** Grant only the necessary permissions to users and services. Regularly review and revoke unnecessary access.
- **Zero Trust Security:** Assume no implicit trust and require verification for every access request, even from within the network.
- **Regular Security Awareness Training:** Educate users about phishing, social engineering, and other tactics used to steal credentials.
- **Monitor for Suspicious Activity:** Use security tools to detect anomalous login attempts, unusual access patterns, or other suspicious behavior.
- **Implement Role-Based Access Control (RBAC):** Define roles with specific permissions and assign users to those roles.
- **Regularly Audit Access Logs:** Review access logs to identify any unauthorized access attempts or suspicious activity.
- **Secure API Access:** Use strong authentication and authorization mechanisms to protect cloud APIs.

By implementing these security practices, organizations can significantly reduce the risk of account hijacking, unauthorized access, and lateral movement in their cloud environments. A layered approach, combining technical controls with user education and strong security policies, is crucial for protecting sensitive data and maintaining a secure cloud environment.

Infrastructure Security in the Cloud

Infrastructure security in the cloud involves protecting the underlying computing resources and network infrastructure that support cloud services. It's a shared responsibility, with the cloud provider securing the physical infrastructure (hardware, data centers) and the customer securing the virtualized infrastructure they deploy *on* that foundation.

Key Components and Security Considerations:

- **Securing Virtual Machines (VMs):** VMs are a fundamental building block of many cloud deployments. Securing them involves:
    - **Hardening:** Configuring VMs securely by disabling unnecessary services, applying security patches, and implementing strong access controls.
    - **Image Management:** Using trusted and up-to-date base images for VM creation. Regularly patching and updating these images.
    - **Security Scanning:** Regularly scanning VMs for vulnerabilities and misconfigurations.
    - **Isolation:** Isolating VMs from each other to prevent lateral movement in case of a compromise.
    - **Monitoring:** Monitoring VM activity for suspicious behavior.
- **Securing Containers:** Containers offer a lightweight and portable way to deploy applications. Securing them requires:
    - **Image Security:** Using trusted container images from reputable registries. Scanning images for vulnerabilities.
    - **Orchestration Security:** Securing the container orchestration platform (e.g., Kubernetes). Implementing access controls and network policies.
    - **Runtime Security:** Monitoring container runtime behavior for suspicious activity.
    - **Resource Limits:** Setting resource limits for containers to prevent resource exhaustion attacks.
- **Securing Serverless Functions:** Serverless functions (e.g., AWS Lambda, Azure Functions) are event-driven compute services. Securing them involves:
    - **Code Security:** Writing secure code and avoiding common vulnerabilities.
    - **Dependency Management:** Managing and securing third-party libraries and dependencies.
    - **Access Control:** Implementing strict access controls to limit who can invoke functions.
    - **Secrets Management:** Securely storing and managing API keys, passwords, and other sensitive information used by functions.
    - **Monitoring:** Monitoring function execution for errors and suspicious activity.
- **Protecting Against DDoS Attacks and Other Network Threats:** Distributed Denial of Service (DDoS) attacks aim to overwhelm a target with traffic, making it unavailable to legitimate users. Protecting against them requires:
    - **DDoS Mitigation Services:** Utilizing cloud-based DDoS mitigation services that can detect and filter malicious traffic.
    - **Web Application Firewalls (WAFs):** Using WAFs to protect web applications from common attacks, such as SQL injection and cross-site scripting.
    - **Network Segmentation:** Segmenting the network to limit the impact of a DDoS attack.
    - **Intrusion Detection/Prevention Systems (IDS/IPS):** Deploying IDS/IPS to

detect and block malicious network traffic.

- Ensuring the Security of Cloud Infrastructure Components: This encompasses various aspects, including:
    - **Network Security:** Securing virtual networks, subnets, and security groups. Implementing firewalls and other network security controls.
    - **Storage Security:** Encrypting data at rest and in transit. Implementing access controls to limit who can access storage resources.
    - **Compute Security:** Securing the underlying compute resources, including virtual machines, containers, and serverless functions.
    - **Management Plane Security:** Securing the cloud management console and APIs used to manage cloud resources. Implementing strong authentication and authorization.

Key Security Practices for Cloud Infrastructure:

- **Shared Responsibility Model:** Clearly define the security responsibilities between the cloud provider and the customer.
- **Security Hardening:** Implement security best practices for all cloud resources.
- **Vulnerability Management:** Regularly scan for vulnerabilities and apply patches.
- **Security Monitoring and Logging:** Monitor cloud infrastructure for suspicious activity and maintain detailed logs.
- **Incident Response Planning:** Develop and test incident response plans for cloud environments.
- **Automation:** Automate security tasks to improve efficiency and reduce human error.

By addressing these infrastructure security considerations, organizations can build more secure and resilient cloud environments. A layered security approach, combining technical controls with strong security policies and continuous monitoring, is essential for protecting cloud infrastructure from evolving cyber threats.

Compliance and Regulatory Requirements: A Critical Component of Cloud Security

Organizations operating in regulated industries must adhere to specific compliance standards and regulations to protect sensitive data and maintain the integrity of their systems. Moving to the cloud adds complexity to compliance efforts, as organizations must ensure their cloud deployments meet these requirements.

Key Considerations:

- **Meeting Industry-Specific Compliance Standards:** Different industries have different compliance requirements. Some key examples include:
    - **HIPAA (Health Insurance Portability and Accountability Act):** Applies to healthcare organizations and requires them to protect the privacy and security

of Protected Health Information (PHI).

- **PCI DSS (Payment Card Industry Data Security Standard):** Applies to organizations that handle credit card transactions and sets requirements for protecting cardholder data.
- **SOX (Sarbanes-Oxley Act):** Applies to publicly traded companies and requires them to maintain accurate financial records and internal controls.
- **GDPR (General Data Protection Regulation):** A European Union regulation that sets strict requirements for data privacy and security. It applies to any organization that collects or processes the personal data of EU residents, regardless of where the organization is located.
- **CCPA (California Consumer Privacy Act):** A California law that grants consumers greater control over their personal data. It has influenced other US states to adopt similar legislation.

- **Data Residency and Sovereignty:** Many regulations require organizations to store data within specific geographic regions or countries. This is known as data residency or data sovereignty. Organizations must ensure that their cloud deployments comply with these requirements.
- **Data Governance:** Implementing strong data governance policies and procedures is essential for compliance. This includes defining roles and responsibilities for data management, establishing data retention policies, and implementing access controls.
- **Audit Trails and Logging:** Maintaining detailed audit trails and logs of system activity is crucial for demonstrating compliance to auditors and regulators. These logs should be secure and tamper-proof.
- **Security Assessments and Penetration Testing:** Regular security assessments and penetration testing are necessary to identify vulnerabilities and ensure that security controls are effective.
- **Vendor Management:** Organizations must also ensure that their cloud providers and other third-party vendors comply with relevant regulations. This includes conducting due diligence on vendors and reviewing their security practices.
- **Demonstrating Compliance to Auditors and Regulators:** Organizations must be able to demonstrate compliance to auditors and regulators. This requires having documented policies and procedures, maintaining accurate records, and being able to provide evidence of compliance.

Key Steps for Achieving and Demonstrating Compliance in the Cloud:

1. **Understand the Requirements:** Identify the specific compliance standards and regulations that apply to your organization.
2. **Conduct a Gap Analysis:** Assess your current security posture and identify any gaps between your current practices and the required standards.
3. **Develop a Compliance Plan:** Create a detailed plan for achieving and maintaining compliance.
4. **Implement Security Controls:** Implement the necessary technical and administrative

controls to meet the compliance requirements.

5. **Monitor and Audit:** Continuously monitor your cloud environment for compliance and conduct regular audits.
6. **Document Everything:** Maintain detailed documentation of your compliance efforts, including policies, procedures, audit logs, and assessment reports.
7. **Engage with Auditors and Regulators:** Be prepared to provide evidence of compliance to auditors and regulators.

Key Considerations:

- **Shared Responsibility Model:** Remember that compliance is a shared responsibility between the cloud provider and the customer. Understand which controls are the responsibility of each party.
- **Cloud Provider Certifications:** Look for cloud providers that have certifications and attestations relevant to your industry and compliance requirements (e.g., ISO 27001, SOC 2).
- **Automation:** Automate compliance tasks where possible to improve efficiency and reduce the risk of human error.

By addressing these compliance and regulatory requirements, organizations can ensure that their cloud deployments meet the necessary standards and protect sensitive data. A proactive and comprehensive approach to compliance is essential for maintaining trust with customers and avoiding regulatory penalties.

Emerging Threats in Cloud Security

- **Cloud-Native Threats:** These threats specifically target the unique characteristics of cloud-native technologies, such as serverless functions and containers.
    - **Serverless Function Vulnerabilities:** Serverless functions, while offering many benefits, also introduce new security challenges. Vulnerabilities in function code, insecure dependencies, misconfigured permissions, or improper secrets management can be exploited by attackers. Because serverless functions are often short-lived and event-driven, traditional security scanning and monitoring tools may not be as effective.
    - **Container Security:** Containers, while providing portability and efficiency, can also be a source of vulnerabilities. Insecure container images, vulnerabilities in the container orchestration platform (like Kubernetes), and misconfigured network policies can be exploited by attackers. The rapid adoption of containers and the complexity of managing them at scale can also increase the risk of security misconfigurations.
- The Rise of Cloud-Based Ransomware and Other Malicious Attacks:
    - **Cloud-Based Ransomware:** Ransomware attacks are increasingly targeting cloud environments. Attackers may exploit vulnerabilities to gain access to

cloud storage, encrypt data, and demand a ransom. The distributed nature of cloud data can make it more challenging to recover from these attacks. Cloud-based backups can also be targeted by attackers.

- **Other Malicious Attacks:** Cloud environments are susceptible to a wide range of other malicious attacks, including:
    - **Data Exfiltration:** Attackers may attempt to steal sensitive data stored in the cloud.
    - **Denial-of-Service (DoS) Attacks:** Attackers may attempt to disrupt cloud services by overwhelming them with traffic.
    - **Cryptojacking:** Attackers may compromise cloud resources to mine cryptocurrency without the owner's knowledge or consent.
    - **API Attacks:** Insecure APIs can be exploited to gain unauthorized access to cloud resources or to steal data.

Key Considerations Related to Emerging Threats

- **Rapid Evolution:** The cloud threat landscape is constantly evolving, requiring organizations to stay up-to-date on the latest threats and vulnerabilities.
- **Lack of Visibility:** Maintaining visibility into cloud-native environments can be challenging, making it difficult to detect and respond to security incidents.
- **Automation:** Automating security tasks and incident response is crucial for keeping pace with the rapid evolution of cloud-native threats.
- **Skills Gap:** The shortage of skilled cloud security professionals makes it difficult for organizations to effectively address these emerging threats.

Key Security Practices to Mitigate Emerging Threats

- **Secure Coding Practices:** Emphasize secure coding practices for serverless functions and containerized applications.
- **Vulnerability Scanning:** Regularly scan serverless functions and container images for vulnerabilities.
- **Runtime Security:** Monitor the runtime behavior of serverless functions and containers for suspicious activity.
- **Access Control:** Implement strong access controls to limit who can access cloud resources.
- **Secrets Management:** Securely store and manage API keys, passwords, and other sensitive information used by serverless functions and containerized applications.
- **Network Security:** Implement network security controls to protect against DDoS attacks and other network threats.
- **Data Backup and Recovery:** Regularly back up data to protect against ransomware attacks and other data loss events.
- **Incident Response Planning:** Develop and test incident response plans for cloud-native environments.
- **Security Automation:** Automate security tasks and incident response to improve

efficiency and reduce human error.

- **Threat Intelligence:** Stay informed about the latest cloud-native threats and vulnerabilities by leveraging threat intelligence feeds.

By understanding these emerging threats and implementing appropriate security measures, organizations can better protect their cloud environments and minimize the risk of attacks. A proactive and comprehensive approach to cloud security is essential for staying ahead of the evolving threat landscape.

Cloud Security Solutions

Let's explore the key solutions available to address the cloud security challenges we've discussed. Cloud security is a multi-faceted area, and effective protection requires a combination of strategies and tools.

Cloud Security Solutions: A Comprehensive Approach

These solutions can be broadly categorized as follows:

1. Foundational Security Practices:
    - **Shared Responsibility Model Understanding:** Clearly define the responsibilities between the cloud provider and the customer. This is the *basis* of effective cloud security.
    - **Security Posture Management:** Regularly assess and improve your cloud security posture. Use cloud security posture management (CSPM) tools to identify misconfigurations and vulnerabilities.
    - **Security Awareness Training:** Educate employees about cloud security best practices, phishing awareness, and other common threats.
    - **Data Governance Policies:** Establish clear policies for data access, usage, retention, and disposal.
    - **Incident Response Planning:** Develop and regularly test incident response plans specific to cloud environments.
2. Data Security Solutions:
    - **Encryption:** Encrypt data both in transit (TLS/SSL) and at rest (using encryption at the storage level). Manage encryption keys securely.
    - **Data Loss Prevention (DLP):** Implement DLP tools to prevent sensitive data from leaving your control.
    - **Data Masking and Tokenization:** Use these techniques to protect sensitive data while still allowing it to be used for testing and development.
    - **Database Security:** Implement database security measures, such as access control,

encryption, and auditing.
- **Cloud Access Security Brokers (CASBs):** CASBs monitor and control access to cloud applications, helping to prevent data breaches and enforce security policies.

3. Identity and Access Management (IAM) Solutions:
    - **Multi-Factor Authentication (MFA):** Require MFA for all cloud accounts, especially privileged accounts.
    - **Strong Password Policies:** Enforce strong password complexity requirements and regular password changes.
    - **Key-Based Authentication and Key Rotation:** Implement **key-based access mechanisms** (such as SSH keys for cloud instances) instead of relying solely on passwords, enhancing security through cryptographic authentication. o Establish policies for **regular key rotation**, ensuring cryptographic keys are changed periodically to reduce the risk of compromise and maintain strong access controls. Securely manage and store keys using dedicated **key management services (KMS)** offered by cloud providers to prevent unauthorized access and enforce lifecycle management best practices.
    - **Principle of Least Privilege:** Grant users only the minimum necessary permissions.
    - **Role-Based Access Control (RBAC):** Use RBAC to manage user access based on roles and responsibilities.
    - **Identity Federation:** Integrate cloud IAM with your on-premises identity systems.
    - **Regular Access Reviews:** Periodically review user permissions and revoke access for former employees or users who no longer need it.
4. Network Security Solutions:
    - **Virtual Private Clouds (VPCs):** Use VPCs to isolate your cloud resources from the public internet and other tenants.
    - **Security Groups:** Implement security groups (firewalls) to control inbound and outbound traffic to your cloud resources.
    - **Web Application Firewalls (WAFs):** Protect web applications from common attacks, such as SQL injection and cross-site scripting.
    - **Intrusion Detection/Prevention Systems (IDS/IPS):** Deploy IDS/IPS to detect and block malicious network traffic.
    - **DDoS Protection:** Utilize cloud-based DDoS mitigation services to protect against distributed denial-of-service attacks.
5. Compute Security Solutions:
    - **Vulnerability Scanning:** Regularly scan virtual machines, containers, and serverless functions for vulnerabilities.
    - **Patch Management:** Implement a robust patch management process to keep systems up-to-date.
    - **Hardening:** Securely configure virtual machines and containers by disabling unnecessary services and applying security best practices.
    - **Container Image Security:** Use trusted container images and scan them for vulnerabilities.

- **Serverless Function Security:** Follow secure coding practices and implement appropriate access controls for serverless functions.
- **Endpoint Security:** Protect endpoints (laptops, mobile devices) that access cloud resources.

6. Security Monitoring and Logging Solutions:
   - **Security Information and Event Management (SIEM):** Use SIEM tools to collect and analyze security logs from various cloud sources.
   - **Cloud Monitoring Tools:** Leverage cloud-native monitoring tools to gain visibility into your cloud environment.
   - **Threat Intelligence:** Integrate threat intelligence feeds to identify and respond to emerging threats.
7. Compliance Solutions:
   - **Compliance Automation Tools:** Use tools to automate compliance checks and generate reports.
   - **Cloud Provider Certifications:** Choose cloud providers that have certifications relevant to your industry and compliance requirements.
   - **Regular Audits:** Conduct regular security audits to ensure compliance.
8. Cloud-Native Security Solutions:
   - **Container Security Platforms:** Use dedicated container security platforms to protect your containerized applications.
   - **Serverless Security Tools:** Leverage serverless security tools to secure your serverless functions.
9. Emerging Technology Security:
   - **AI/ML for Security:** Use AI/ML to enhance threat detection and incident response.
   - **Blockchain for Security:** Explore the potential of blockchain for securing data and identities.

Key Considerations:

- **Multi-Layered Security:** Implement a multi-layered security approach, combining different security solutions to provide comprehensive protection.
- **Automation:** Automate security tasks where possible to improve efficiency and reduce human error.
- **Continuous Monitoring:** Continuously monitor your cloud environment for security threats and vulnerabilities.
- **Skills Gap:** Address the cloud security skills gap by training your staff or hiring experienced cloud security professionals.

By implementing these cloud security solutions, organizations can significantly improve their security posture and protect their data and applications in the cloud. A proactive and comprehensive approach is essential for staying ahead of evolving cyber threats and ensuring a secure cloud environment.

Identity and Access Management (IAM)

You're focusing on a critical area of cloud security: Identity and Access Management (IAM). It's often said that IAM is the new perimeter, and for good reason. Let's break down the key aspects you've highlighted:

Identity and Access Management (IAM) in the Cloud: Protecting the Keys to the Kingdom
IAM is the process of managing user identities and their access to resources. In the cloud, this means controlling who can access your cloud environment and what they can do once they're in. Robust IAM is fundamental to cloud security.

Key IAM Practices:

- **Implementing Multi-Factor Authentication (MFA):** MFA adds an extra layer of security beyond just a password. It requires users to provide multiple forms of authentication, such as:
    - Something you know (password)
    - Something you have (code from a mobile app, hardware token)
    - Something you are (biometric scan)

MFA makes it significantly harder for attackers to gain access even if they have stolen a password. It should be *mandatory* for all privileged accounts (administrators) and highly recommended for all users.

- **Least Privilege Access Control:** This principle dictates that users should only be granted the minimum necessary permissions to perform their job functions. It limits the "blast radius" of a compromised account. If an attacker gains access to an account with limited privileges, they will have less opportunity to cause widespread damage. Implementing least privilege involves:
    - Defining roles with specific permissions.
    - Assigning users to roles based on their job requirements.
    - Regularly reviewing and revoking unnecessary permissions.
- Regular Password Rotations and Security Assessments:
    - **Password Rotations:** While MFA is the most effective control, strong password policies are still important. Enforce password complexity requirements (minimum length, mix of characters) and regular password changes. However, *frequent* password rotations (e.g., every 30 days) are less emphasized now in favor of stronger, unique passwords and MFA due to studies showing less benefit and user frustration.
    - **Security Assessments:** Regularly assess the security of your IAM system. This includes:
        - **Vulnerability Scanning:** Scanning for vulnerabilities in IAM-related software and systems.
        - **Penetration Testing:** Simulating attacks to identify weaknesses in your IAM controls.
        - **Access Reviews:** Periodically reviewing user permissions to ensure they are still appropriate and revoke access for former employees or

users who no longer need it.

- **Auditing:** Regularly auditing IAM logs to identify any suspicious activity or unauthorized access attempts.

Additional Important IAM Considerations

- **Identity Federation:** Integrating your cloud IAM with your on-premises identity systems can simplify user management and improve security.
- **Centralized IAM:** Using a centralized IAM system can make it easier to manage user identities and access across multiple cloud environments and on-premises systems.
- **Privileged Access Management (PAM):** PAM solutions provide enhanced security for privileged accounts. They typically include features such as:
    - Vaulting and rotating privileged credentials.
    - Session recording and auditing.
    - Just-in-time access granting.
- **Monitoring and Alerting:** Monitor IAM logs for suspicious activity and set up alerts for unusual login attempts or other anomalous behavior.
- **User Lifecycle Management:** Have a process for onboarding and offboarding users, including promptly revoking access for terminated employees.
- **Security Awareness Training:** Train users about phishing, social engineering, and other tactics used to steal credentials.

By implementing these IAM best practices, organizations can significantly improve their cloud security posture and protect against unauthorized access to their cloud resources. A layered approach, combining strong technical controls with user education and robust security policies, is essential for effective IAM in the cloud.

Data Encryption:

Data encryption is a cornerstone of cloud security. It's essential for protecting sensitive information both as it travels across networks and when it's stored in cloud environments. Let's break down the key aspects you've highlighted:

Data Encryption: Protecting Data's Confidentiality

Encryption transforms data into an unreadable format (ciphertext), making it unusable to anyone without the decryption key. It's a crucial control for protecting data confidentiality.

Key Concepts and Practices:

- Encrypting Data in Transit and at Rest:
    - **In Transit:** Data being transmitted over a network (e.g., between a user's browser and a cloud server, or between cloud services) should be encrypted. The standard protocol for this is TLS (Transport Layer Security), formerly known as SSL (Secure Sockets Layer). TLS encrypts the communication channel, preventing eavesdropping and tampering.

    - **At Rest:** Data stored in cloud storage (databases, object storage, file systems) should also be encrypted. This protects the data even if the storage is compromised (e.g., a physical drive is stolen, or an attacker gains unauthorized access). Encryption at rest is typically handled by the cloud provider (at the storage level), but you can also implement application-level encryption for added security.
- **Key Management:** Encryption is only as strong as the security of the encryption keys. Proper key management is *essential*. This involves:
    - **Generating Strong Keys:** Using cryptographically secure methods to generate keys.
    - **Storing Keys Securely:** Protecting keys from unauthorized access. Cloud providers offer key management services (KMS) that provide secure key storage and management.
    - **Key Rotation:** Regularly rotating keys to limit the impact of a potential compromise.
    - **Access Control:** Controlling who has access to encryption keys.
- **Data Loss Prevention (DLP):** DLP goes beyond just encryption. It aims to prevent sensitive data from leaving your control, even if it's accidentally or intentionally mishandled. DLP solutions can:
    - **Identify Sensitive Data:** Scan data (both in transit and at rest) to identify sensitive information (PII, PHI, financial data).
    - **Prevent Data Exfiltration:** Block or alert on attempts to transfer sensitive data to unauthorized locations (e.g., personal email, USB drives).
    - **Monitor Data Access:** Track who is accessing sensitive data and how it is being used.
- **Data Masking and Tokenization:** These techniques protect sensitive data by replacing it with a masked or tokenized value. This allows the data to be used for testing, development, or analytics without exposing the actual sensitive information.
    - **Data Masking:** Replaces sensitive data with realistic but fictional data. For example, a credit card number might be masked to show only the last four digits.
    - **Tokenization:** Replaces sensitive data with a randomly generated token. The token can be used in place of the actual data, and the mapping between the token and the real data is stored securely.

Key Considerations for Data Encryption:

- **Choosing the Right Encryption Algorithms:** Use strong and well-vetted encryption algorithms.
- **Performance Impact:** Encryption can have a performance impact, so it's important to choose encryption methods that balance security with performance.
- **Compliance Requirements:** Ensure your encryption practices meet relevant regulatory requirements (e.g., HIPAA, PCI DSS).

- **Key Management is Crucial:** The security of your encryption is entirely dependent on the security of your keys. Invest in a robust key management solution.

By implementing these data encryption and related practices, organizations can significantly enhance the protection of their sensitive data in the cloud. A layered approach, combining encryption with access control, DLP, and other security measures, is essential for a robust data security strategy.

Virtual Private Cloud (VPC) Security

You're focusing on a crucial aspect of cloud security: Virtual Private Cloud (VPC) security. A VPC is your own private slice of the cloud provider's infrastructure, and securing it is paramount. Let's break down the key elements you've highlighted:

Virtual Private Cloud (VPC) Security: Building Your Secure Cloud Perimeter
A VPC is a logically isolated section of the cloud provider's network where you can launch your cloud resources (virtual machines, databases, etc.) in a virtual network that you define. It's like having your own private data center in the cloud.

Key VPC Security Components and Practices

- **Network Segmentation and Access Control:** This is a fundamental principle of security, and it's essential within a VPC.
    - **Subnetting:** Divide your VPC into smaller subnets. This allows you to isolate different parts of your application and apply different security rules to each subnet. For example, you might have separate subnets for web servers, application servers, and databases.
    - **Security Groups:** Act as virtual firewalls for your instances (virtual machines). You define rules to control inbound and outbound traffic at the instance level.
    - **Network Access Control Lists (NACLs):** Provide an additional layer of network traffic control at the subnet level. NACLs are stateless, meaning they evaluate traffic based on the rules you define, regardless of previous connections.
- Firewalls and Intrusion Detection Systems (IDS):
    - **Firewalls:** Control network traffic based on predefined rules. VPCs use security groups and NACLs as firewalls. You can also deploy web application firewalls (WAFs) to protect web applications from common attacks.
    - **Intrusion Detection/Prevention Systems (IDS/IPS):** Monitor network traffic for malicious activity. IDS alert you to suspicious activity, while IPS can automatically block or mitigate attacks. You can deploy IDS/IPS within your VPC to monitor traffic flowing between subnets or to protect specific applications.
- **VPN Connections for Secure Remote Access:** A Virtual Private Network (VPN)

creates an encrypted tunnel between your on-premises network and your VPC. This allows authorized users to securely access cloud resources from your corporate network. VPNs are also used to connect different VPCs together. There are two main types:

- **Site-to-Site VPN:** Connects your entire on-premises network to your VPC.
- **Client VPN:** Allows individual users to connect securely to your VPC from anywhere.

Additional Important VPC Security Considerations

- **Route Tables:** Control how traffic is routed within your VPC and to/from the internet. Properly configured route tables are crucial for network segmentation and security.
- **Internet Gateways:** Allow your VPC to connect to the public internet. Securely configure internet gateways to prevent unauthorized access.
- **NAT Gateways:** Allow instances in your VPC to connect to the internet without exposing their public IP addresses. This enhances security and privacy.
- **DNS Security:** Protect your DNS records from tampering and ensure that your DNS servers are secure.
- **Monitoring and Logging:** Monitor network traffic within your VPC for suspicious activity and maintain detailed logs.
- **Regular Security Assessments:** Conduct regular security assessments and penetration testing to identify vulnerabilities in your VPC configuration.

Key Security Practices for VPCs:

- **Principle of Least Privilege:** Apply the principle of least privilege to network access, granting only the necessary permissions to resources and services.
- **Defense in Depth:** Implement multiple layers of security to protect your VPC.
- **Security Automation:** Automate security tasks where possible to improve efficiency and reduce human error.
- **Regular Security Audits:** Conduct regular security audits to ensure your VPC is configured securely.

By implementing these VPC security best practices, organizations can create a secure and isolated environment for their cloud resources. A well-designed and secured VPC is a fundamental building block of a robust cloud security strategy.

Cloud Security Posture Management (CSPM)

You're focusing on a crucial and increasingly important area of cloud security: Cloud Security Posture Management (CSPM). With the complexity and dynamic nature of cloud environments, having a way to continuously assess and improve your security is essential.

Cloud Security Posture Management (CSPM): Keeping Your Cloud Secure

CSPM refers to the continuous process of monitoring, assessing, and improving the security posture of your cloud environments. It helps organizations identify and remediate security misconfigurations, vulnerabilities, and compliance gaps.

Key Components and Capabilities of CSPM:

- **Continuous Monitoring and Assessment:** CSPM tools continuously monitor your cloud resources (virtual machines, storage, networks, IAM configurations, etc.) for security misconfigurations and compliance violations. They use automated checks and rules to identify potential issues.
- **Identifying Security Misconfigurations:** CSPM tools can detect a wide range of misconfigurations, such as:
    - Open security groups (firewall rules) that allow unauthorized access.
    - Unencrypted storage buckets containing sensitive data.
    - IAM roles with excessive permissions.
    - Missing security patches.
    - Non-compliant configurations (e.g., not meeting industry standards or regulatory requirements).
- **Remediating Security Misconfigurations:** CSPM tools often provide automated remediation capabilities, allowing you to quickly fix identified misconfigurations. They may offer suggestions for remediation or even automatically apply fixes.
- **Compliance Validation:** CSPM tools can check your cloud configurations against various compliance frameworks and industry best practices (e.g., CIS Benchmarks, NIST Cybersecurity Framework, HIPAA, PCI DSS, GDPR). They can generate reports to demonstrate compliance to auditors.
- **Visibility and Reporting:** CSPM tools provide a centralized view of your cloud security posture across multiple cloud environments. They offer dashboards and reports to visualize security risks and track remediation efforts.
- **Threat Intelligence Integration:** Some CSPM tools integrate with threat intelligence feeds to identify and prioritize risks based on the latest threat landscape.
- **Multi-Cloud Support:** Many organizations use multiple cloud providers. CSPM tools can provide a unified view of security posture across these different environments.

Benefits of CSPM:

- **Improved Security Posture:** CSPM helps organizations proactively identify and address security risks, reducing the likelihood of breaches.
- **Reduced Risk of Misconfigurations:** Automated monitoring and assessment help prevent misconfigurations, a common source of cloud vulnerabilities.
- **Enhanced Compliance:** CSPM simplifies compliance efforts by automating compliance checks and generating reports.
- **Faster Remediation:** Automated remediation capabilities enable organizations to quickly fix security misconfigurations.
- **Increased Visibility:** CSPM provides a centralized view of cloud security posture across multiple environments.
- **Cost Savings:** By preventing security breaches and simplifying compliance, CSPM can

help organizations save money.

Key Considerations for Choosing a CSPM Solution:

- **Coverage:** Ensure the CSPM tool covers all the cloud services and resources you are using.
- **Accuracy:** Choose a tool that provides accurate and reliable security assessments.
- **Automation:** Look for a tool that offers automated remediation capabilities.
- **Integration:** Select a tool that integrates with your existing security tools and workflows.
- **Reporting and Dashboards:** Choose a tool that provides clear and actionable reports and dashboards.
- **Scalability:** Ensure the tool can scale to meet your needs as your cloud usage grows.

Key Practices for Effective CSPM:

- **Continuous Monitoring:** Regularly monitor your cloud environment using CSPM tools.
- **Prioritize Remediation:** Focus on remediating the most critical security misconfigurations first.
- **Automate Remediation:** Automate remediation tasks where possible.
- **Integrate with DevOps:** Integrate CSPM into your DevOps pipeline to "shift left" security and catch issues early.
- **Regularly Review and Update:** Regularly review and update your CSPM policies and rules to keep pace with the evolving threat landscape.

By implementing a robust CSPM program, organizations can significantly improve their cloud security posture and reduce the risk of security incidents. It's an essential component of a comprehensive cloud security strategy.

Cloud Workload Protection Platforms (CWPPs)

You're focusing on a critical area of cloud security: Cloud Workload Protection Platforms (CWPPs). As workloads become more diverse and dynamic in the cloud, having specialized protection for them is essential.

Cloud Workload Protection Platforms (CWPPs): Protecting Your Cloud Workloads CWPPs are security solutions specifically designed to protect workloads (virtual machines, containers, serverless functions) running in cloud environments. They provide a range of security capabilities to detect and respond to threats in real-time.

Key Capabilities of CWPPs:

- **Workload Hardening:** CWPPs help secure workloads by:

- Vulnerability Scanning: Identifying vulnerabilities in operating systems, applications, and container images.
- Configuration Assessment: Checking workload configurations against security best practices and compliance benchmarks.
- Patch Management: Automating or assisting with the patching of vulnerabilities.

- **Runtime Protection:** CWPPs monitor workload runtime behavior for suspicious activity, such as:
  - Malware Detection: Detecting and blocking malware execution.
  - Anomaly Detection: Identifying unusual behavior that may indicate an attack.
  - File Integrity Monitoring: Tracking changes to critical files.
  - Behavioral Analysis: Analyzing workload behavior to detect malicious activity.
- **Threat Detection and Response:** CWPPs can detect and respond to threats in real-time, including:
  - Intrusion Detection/Prevention: Detecting and blocking malicious network traffic.
  - Security Incident Response: Automating or assisting with incident response actions.
- **Container Security:** CWPPs provide specialized security for containers, including:
  - Image Scanning: Scanning container images for vulnerabilities.
  - Runtime Security: Monitoring container runtime behavior.
  - Orchestration Security: Securing the container orchestration platform (e.g., Kubernetes).
- **Serverless Security:** CWPPs can also secure serverless functions by:
  - Code Analysis: Analyzing function code for vulnerabilities.
  - Dependency Management: Managing and securing function dependencies.
  - Access Control: Implementing strict access controls for functions.
- **Visibility and Control:** CWPPs provide visibility into workload activity and security posture, allowing you to monitor and manage security risks.
- **Compliance:** CWPPs can help organizations meet compliance requirements by providing security controls and generating reports.

Benefits of CWPPs:

- **Improved Workload Security:** CWPPs provide comprehensive protection for cloud workloads, reducing the risk of security breaches.
- **Real-time Threat Detection and Response:** CWPPs can detect and respond to threats in real-time, minimizing the impact of attacks.
- **Enhanced Visibility:** CWPPs provide visibility into workload activity and security posture, allowing you to monitor and manage security risks.
- **Simplified Security Management:** CWPPs can simplify security management by providing a centralized platform for protecting workloads.
- **Improved Compliance:** CWPPs can help organizations meet compliance

requirements.

Key Considerations for Choosing a CWPP:

- **Workload Coverage:** Ensure the CWPP supports the types of workloads you are running (VMs, containers, serverless functions).
- **Integration:** Choose a CWPP that integrates with your existing security tools and workflows.
- **Automation:** Look for a CWPP that offers automated remediation capabilities.
- **Performance:** Ensure the CWPP does not negatively impact workload performance.
- **Scalability:** Choose a CWPP that can scale to meet your needs as your cloud usage grows.

Key Practices for Effective CWPP Use:

- **Deploy CWPPs Early:** Implement CWPPs as early as possible in the cloud adoption process.
- **Configure Properly:** Properly configure CWPPs to meet your specific security needs.
- **Continuously Monitor:** Continuously monitor workload activity and security posture using CWPPs.
- **Automate Responses:** Automate security incident response actions where possible.
- **Integrate with Other Security Tools:** Integrate CWPPs with other security tools, such as SIEM and threat intelligence platforms.

By implementing CWPPs and following best practices, organizations can significantly improve the security of their cloud workloads and protect against evolving cyber threats. CWPPs are an essential component of a comprehensive cloud security strategy.

Cloud Security Information and Event Management (SIEM):
You're focusing on a crucial aspect of cloud security: Cloud Security Information and Event Management (SIEM). With the volume and variety of security events in cloud environments, having a centralized system to analyze and respond to them is essential.

Cloud Security Information and Event Management (SIEM): Your Security Nerve Center
Cloud SIEM solutions are designed to collect, analyze, and manage security logs and events from various cloud sources. They provide a centralized platform for security monitoring, threat detection, and incident response in cloud environments.

Key Capabilities of Cloud SIEM:

- **Centralized Logging and Monitoring:** Cloud SIEMs collect logs and events from a wide range of cloud sources, including:
    - Cloud provider logs (e.g., AWS CloudTrail, Azure Activity Log, Google Cloud Audit Logs)
    - Virtual machine logs

  - Container logs
  - Serverless function logs
  - Security tool logs (e.g., firewalls, intrusion detection systems)
  - Application logs
  - User activity logs

This centralized logging and monitoring provides a comprehensive view of security events across your cloud environment.

- **Threat Detection:** Cloud SIEMs use various techniques to detect security threats, including:
  - Correlation: Correlating events from different sources to identify complex attacks.
  - Anomaly Detection: Identifying unusual behavior that may indicate a security incident.
  - Rule-Based Detection: Detecting known attack patterns based on predefined rules.
  - Machine Learning: Using machine learning to identify new and evolving threats.
- **Incident Response:** Cloud SIEMs facilitate incident response by:
  - Providing alerts and notifications about security incidents.
  - Enabling security analysts to investigate incidents.
  - Automating incident response actions (e.g., isolating compromised instances).
  - Generating reports and dashboards to track incident response progress.
- **Compliance:** Cloud SIEMs can help organizations meet compliance requirements by providing audit trails and reports.
- **Threat Intelligence Integration:** Many cloud SIEMs integrate with threat intelligence feeds to identify and prioritize threats based on the latest threat landscape.
- **User and Entity Behavior Analytics (UEBA):** Some SIEMs include UEBA capabilities to detect insider threats and compromised accounts by analyzing user and entity behavior.

Benefits of Cloud SIEM

- **Improved Threat Detection:** Cloud SIEMs can detect a wider range of threats than traditional security monitoring tools.
- **Faster Incident Response:** Cloud SIEMs can automate incident response actions, reducing the time it takes to contain and remediate security incidents.
- **Enhanced Visibility:** Cloud SIEMs provide a centralized view of security events across your cloud environment.
- **Improved Compliance:** Cloud SIEMs can help organizations meet compliance requirements.
- **Reduced Security Costs:** By automating security tasks and improving threat detection, cloud SIEMs can help organizations reduce security costs.

Key Considerations for Choosing a Cloud SIEM

- **Data Ingestion:** Consider the volume and variety of logs and events your SIEM needs to ingest.
- **Scalability:** Choose a SIEM that can scale to meet your needs as your cloud usage grows.
- **Integration:** Ensure the SIEM integrates with your existing security tools and workflows.
- **Analytics and Reporting:** Select a SIEM that provides robust analytics and reporting capabilities.
- **Threat Intelligence:** Look for a SIEM that integrates with threat intelligence feeds.
- **Cost:** Consider the cost of the SIEM, including licensing fees and operational costs.

Key Practices for Effective Cloud SIEM Use

- **Define Use Cases:** Identify the specific security use cases you want to address with your SIEM.
- **Configure Properly:** Properly configure the SIEM to collect and analyze the relevant logs and events.
- **Tune Detection Rules:** Regularly tune detection rules to minimize false positives and ensure accurate threat detection.
- **Automate Responses:** Automate incident response actions where possible.
- **Integrate with Other Security Tools:** Integrate the SIEM with other security tools, such as threat intelligence platforms and SOAR solutions.
- **Regularly Review and Update:** Regularly review and update the SIEM configuration and detection rules to keep pace with the evolving threat landscape.

By implementing a robust cloud SIEM solution and following best practices, organizations can significantly improve their ability to detect and respond to security threats in their cloud environments. A cloud SIEM is a critical component of a comprehensive cloud security strategy.

The Role of Emerging Technologies

Emerging technologies are rapidly changing the cybersecurity landscape, offering both new opportunities for defense and new avenues for attack. Here's a look at some of the key players:

1. Artificial Intelligence (AI) and Machine Learning (ML)

- **Defensive AI/ML:** These technologies can analyze massive datasets of security events, user behavior, and network traffic to identify anomalies, predict threats, and automate incident response. They can also be used to strengthen algorithms, making them more difficult to break.

- **Offensive AI/ML:** Attackers are also leveraging AI/ML to create more sophisticated attacks, such as AI-powered phishing emails, malware that can evade detection, and deepfakes for social engineering.

2. Blockchain
   - **Enhanced Security:** Blockchain's decentralized and immutable nature can enhance security in several ways:
     - **Secure Data Sharing:** Enables secure and transparent sharing of threat intelligence between organizations.
     - **Decentralized Identity Management:** Empowers individuals to control their digital identities, reducing reliance on vulnerable centralized systems.
     - **Supply Chain Security:** Tracks products and materials throughout the supply chain to prevent counterfeiting and ensure authenticity.
3. Quantum Computing
   - **The Double-Edged Sword:** Quantum computing has the potential to break many of the encryption algorithms that currently secure our systems. This poses a significant threat to cybersecurity.
   - **Quantum-Resistant Cryptography:** However, quantum computing is also driving the development of new, quantum-resistant encryption algorithms that can protect data in the age of quantum computing.
4. Internet of Things (IoT) Security
   - **Expanding Attack Surface:** The proliferation of IoT devices has dramatically expanded the attack surface, as many of these devices have weak security and can be easily compromised.
   - **IoT Security Solutions:** Emerging technologies are being developed to address IoT security challenges, such as device authentication, secure communication protocols, and vulnerability management platforms.
5. 5G Network Security
   - **New Security Challenges:** 5G networks offer increased speed and connectivity, but they also introduce new security challenges, such as securing edge computing devices and protecting against new types of attacks.
   - **5G Security Solutions:** Emerging technologies like network slicing, edge security, and AI-powered threat detection are being developed to secure 5G networks.
6. Cloud Security Technologies
   - **Securing Cloud Environments:** As organizations increasingly rely on cloud services, new technologies are emerging to address cloud-specific security challenges, such as:
     - Cloud Security Posture Management (CSPM)
     - Cloud Workload Protection Platforms (CWPP)
     - Cloud Access Security Brokers (CASBs)
7. Biometric and Behavioral Authentication
   - **Enhanced Authentication:** Biometric authentication (fingerprint, facial recognition) and behavioral biometrics (analyzing user behavior patterns) offer more secure alternatives to traditional passwords.

8. Zero Trust Security
    - **Shifting Security Paradigms:** Zero trust is a security framework that assumes no implicit trust and requires verification for every access request, regardless of whether the user is inside or outside the network. It's becoming increasingly important in the cloud era.
9. Automation and Orchestration
    - **Improving Security Efficiency:** Automation and orchestration technologies can help organizations automate security tasks, such as threat detection, incident response, and vulnerability management, improving efficiency and reducing human error.
10. Cybersecurity Mesh
    - **Interconnected Security:** A cybersecurity mesh is a distributed security architecture that connects different security tools and controls, enabling them to work together more effectively.

Key Considerations:

- **Staying Ahead of the Curve:** Organizations need to stay informed about emerging technologies and their potential impact on cybersecurity.
- **Balancing Innovation and Risk:** Adopting new technologies can introduce new risks, so it's important to carefully assess the security implications before implementing them.
- **Addressing the Skills Gap:** The cybersecurity industry faces a skills gap, and organizations need to invest in training and development to ensure they have the expertise to use these emerging technologies effectively.

Emerging technologies are transforming the cybersecurity landscape, offering both new tools for defense and new challenges to overcome. By understanding these technologies and their implications, organizations can better protect themselves against evolving cyber threats.

Artificial Intelligence (AI) and Machine Learning (ML) in Cloud Security

In this section we are overseeing the beautiful intersection of my previous chapter (Chapter 2) on AI in Cybersecurity space along with Cloud security.

AI and ML in Cloud Security: A Powerful Partnership

AI and ML are transforming cloud security by enabling organizations to analyze massive amounts of data, identify patterns, and automate security tasks. This is crucial in the dynamic and complex world of cloud environments.

Key Applications of AI/ML in Cloud Security:

- Anomaly Detection and Threat Intelligence:
    - **Anomaly Detection:** AI/ML algorithms can analyze network traffic, user

behavior, and system logs to identify anomalies that may indicate a security threat. They can learn the "normal" patterns of activity and flag deviations from those patterns.
  - **Threat Intelligence:** AI/ML can process and analyze threat intelligence data from various sources to identify new and emerging threats. This information can be used to proactively protect cloud environments.
- Automated Threat Hunting and Incident Response:
  - **Threat Hunting:** AI/ML can automate the process of threat hunting, proactively searching for hidden threats within cloud environments. This can help organizations identify and respond to attacks before they cause significant damage.
  - **Incident Response:** AI/ML can automate incident response actions, such as isolating compromised instances, blocking malicious traffic, and resetting user passwords. This can significantly reduce the time it takes to contain and remediate security incidents.
- Predictive Analytics for Proactive Threat Mitigation:
  - **Predictive Analytics:** AI/ML can use historical data and threat intelligence to predict future attacks. This allows organizations to proactively strengthen their defenses and mitigate potential threats before they occur.
  - **Proactive Threat Mitigation:** Based on predictive analytics, organizations can take proactive steps to improve their security posture, such as patching vulnerabilities, strengthening access controls, and implementing additional security measures.

Specific Examples of AI/ML in Cloud Security:

- **Malware Detection:** AI/ML can be used to detect malware in cloud storage and network traffic by analyzing file characteristics and behavior.
- **Intrusion Detection:** AI/ML can monitor network traffic for malicious activity and identify intrusion attempts.
- **User Behavior Analytics (UBA):** AI/ML can analyze user behavior to detect insider threats and compromised accounts.
- **Security Automation:** AI/ML can automate security tasks, such as vulnerability scanning, patch management, and incident response.
- **Phishing Detection:** AI/ML can analyze emails and websites to identify phishing attempts.

Benefits of AI/ML in Cloud Security:

- **Improved Threat Detection:** AI/ML can detect a wider range of threats than traditional security tools.
- **Faster Incident Response:** AI/ML can automate incident response actions, reducing the time it takes to contain and remediate security incidents.
- **Proactive Security:** AI/ML can help organizations proactively identify and mitigate

threats before they occur.
- **Increased Efficiency:** AI/ML can automate security tasks, freeing up security personnel to focus on more strategic initiatives.

Key Considerations for Implementing AI/ML in Cloud Security:
- **Data Quality:** AI/ML models are only as good as the data they are trained on. Ensure you have high-quality data to train your models.
- **Model Training and Tuning:** AI/ML models need to be regularly trained and tuned to maintain their accuracy.
- **Explainability:** It's important to understand how AI/ML models make decisions. This can help build trust in the technology and ensure that it is being used responsibly.
- **Skills Gap:** Implementing and managing AI/ML security solutions requires specialized expertise.

By effectively leveraging AI and ML, organizations can significantly enhance their cloud security posture and better protect against evolving cyber threats. These technologies are becoming increasingly essential for securing the complex and dynamic world of cloud computing.

Blockchain in Cloud Security

While still relatively nascent in its widespread application, blockchain's unique characteristics offer some compelling advantages in specific areas. In this we are seeing the interesting intersection of my previous chapter (Chapter 3) of Blockchain and Cybersecurity and Cloud computing and how they interact together to build a compelling dialogue on "Blockchain in Cloud security".

Blockchain in Cloud Security: Enhancing Trust and Security
Blockchain, with its decentralized, immutable, and transparent nature, can address some key challenges in cloud security. It's not a silver bullet, but it can be a valuable tool in specific use cases.
Key Applications of Blockchain in Cloud Security:
- Secure Data Storage and Sharing:
  - **Decentralized Storage:** Blockchain can be used in conjunction with decentralized storage solutions (like IPFS or Filecoin) to create highly resilient and tamper-proof data storage. Data is distributed across a network of nodes, making it much harder for attackers to steal or corrupt.
  - **Secure Data Sharing:** Blockchain can enable secure and auditable data sharing between multiple parties. Permissions can be managed on the blockchain, ensuring that only authorized individuals or organizations can access specific data. This is particularly useful in industries like healthcare or finance where data sharing is essential but must be carefully controlled.

- Decentralized Identity and Access Management (IAM):
    - **Self-Sovereign Identity:** Blockchain can empower individuals to manage their own digital identities. Users can create and control their identities (using Decentralized Identifiers - DIDs) and selectively share verifiable credentials (VCs) with cloud services. This reduces reliance on centralized identity providers, which can be single points of failure.
    - **Decentralized Authentication:** Blockchain can facilitate decentralized authentication, where users can prove their identity without relying on a central authority.
- Immutable Audit Trails and Enhanced Transparency:
    - **Immutable Audit Trails:** Blockchain's immutability makes it ideal for creating tamper-proof audit trails. All security-related events and actions can be recorded on the blockchain, providing a highly reliable record for investigations and compliance purposes. This makes it significantly harder for malicious actors to cover their tracks.
    - **Enhanced Transparency:** For permissioned blockchains (where membership is controlled), the transparent nature of the ledger can enhance transparency and accountability. Authorized parties can view the audit trail, promoting trust and facilitating collaboration.

Specific Examples of Blockchain Use Cases in Cloud Security:

- **Securing IoT Devices:** Blockchain can be used to manage the identities and secure the communication of IoT devices connected to cloud platforms.
- **Supply Chain Security:** Tracking products and components on a blockchain can help prevent counterfeiting and ensure the integrity of the supply chain. This is relevant to cloud infrastructure when hardware components or software updates need to be verified.
- **DNS Security:** Decentralized DNS systems, sometimes built on blockchain, can be more resistant to DNS spoofing and other attacks that redirect users to malicious websites.
- **Vulnerability Disclosure:** A blockchain-based system can create a secure and transparent platform for vulnerability disclosure, allowing researchers to report vulnerabilities without fear of reprisal.

Key Considerations and Challenges:

- **Scalability:** Blockchain technology can be slow and resource-intensive, which can limit its applicability in some situations.
- **Complexity:** Implementing blockchain-based solutions can be complex and require specialized expertise.
- **Integration:** Integrating blockchain with existing cloud systems can be challenging.
- **Security of the Blockchain itself:** While blockchain enhances security in certain areas, the blockchain itself can be vulnerable to attacks (e.g., 51% attacks, smart contract vulnerabilities). It's important to use robust and well-vetted blockchain platforms.

- **Privacy:** While blockchain can enhance transparency, it's important to carefully consider how data is stored and shared to avoid unintentionally revealing sensitive information.
- **Regulatory Uncertainty:** The regulatory landscape surrounding blockchain is still evolving, which can create uncertainty for organizations considering its use.

Despite these challenges, blockchain has the potential to play a valuable role in enhancing specific aspects of cloud security. As the technology matures and addresses its scalability and other limitations, we can expect to see wider adoption of blockchain-based security solutions in the cloud. It's important to remember that blockchain is not a replacement for other security measures but rather a complementary technology that can enhance certain aspects of a comprehensive cloud security strategy.

Future of Cloud Security

The future of cloud security is dynamic and will be shaped by evolving technologies, threat landscapes, and business needs. Here are some key trends and predictions:

1. Increased Automation and AI/ML:
    - **Proactive Security:** AI/ML will play an even greater role in proactive threat detection, prediction, and automated incident response. We'll see more sophisticated anomaly detection, behavioral analytics, and predictive threat modeling.
    - **Automated Remediation:** Automation will be crucial for quickly addressing security misconfigurations, vulnerabilities, and incidents at cloud scale. "Self-healing" infrastructure will become more prevalent.
    - **AI-Driven Threat Hunting:** AI-powered threat hunting will become more sophisticated, enabling security teams to proactively search for hidden threats within cloud environments.
2. Serverless Security:
    - **Specialized Protection:** As serverless computing (functions, FaaS) becomes more widespread, we'll see the development of more specialized security tools and techniques to protect these environments.
    - **Shift-Left Security:** Security will be "shifted left" into the development process for serverless functions, ensuring security is built-in from the start.
3. Container Security Maturation:
    - **Integrated Security:** Container security will become more integrated with the container lifecycle, from image creation to runtime.
    - **Kubernetes Security:** Securing Kubernetes environments will be a top priority, with a focus on access control, network policies, and vulnerability management.
4. Zero Trust Dominance:
    - **Perimeterless Security:** The Zero Trust security model will become the dominant approach, with a focus on verifying every access request, regardless of location.
    - **Microsegmentation:** Microsegmentation will be used to isolate workloads and limit the "blast radius" of security breaches.

5. Cloud-Native Security Platforms:
    - **Consolidated Security:** We'll see the emergence of more comprehensive cloud-native security platforms that integrate various security capabilities (CSPM, CWPP, SIEM) into a single platform.
    - **API Security:** API security will be a major focus, as APIs become increasingly critical for cloud-native applications.
6. Cybersecurity Mesh Architectures:
    - **Interconnected Security:** Cybersecurity mesh architectures will become more prevalent, connecting disparate security tools and controls to enable them to work together more effectively.
7. Quantum-Resistant Cryptography:
    - **Preparing for the Future:** Organizations will begin transitioning to quantum-resistant cryptography to protect their data from future quantum computing attacks.
8. DevSecOps Integration:
    - **Security in the Development Pipeline:** Security will be fully integrated into the DevOps pipeline (DevSecOps), ensuring that security is considered throughout the software development lifecycle.
9. Data Security and Privacy:
    - **Enhanced Data Protection:** Data security and privacy will remain top priorities, with a focus on encryption, data loss prevention, and compliance with regulations like GDPR and CCPA.
    - **Privacy-Preserving Technologies:** Privacy-enhancing technologies (PETs) like homomorphic encryption and differential privacy will become more widely adopted.
10. Skills Gap and Talent Development:
    - **Addressing the Shortage:** The cybersecurity skills gap will continue to be a challenge, and organizations will need to invest in training and development to build their cloud security expertise.
    - **Automation and Managed Services:** Automation and managed security services will play a crucial role in addressing the skills gap.
11. Shared Responsibility Model Clarity:
    - **Clearer Boundaries:** Cloud providers and customers will work together to define clearer boundaries and responsibilities within the shared responsibility model.
    - **Standardized Frameworks:** Industry standards and frameworks will emerge to provide greater clarity on shared responsibilities.
12. Increased Regulatory Scrutiny:
    - **Evolving Regulations:** Governments and regulatory bodies will continue to increase their scrutiny of cloud security practices, leading to new regulations and compliance requirements.
13. Focus on Supply Chain Security:
    - **Securing the Ecosystem:** Organizations will place greater emphasis on securing their cloud supply chains, ensuring that third-party vendors and partners meet their security requirements.

14. Security Orchestration, Automation, and Response (SOAR):

- **Streamlined Incident Response:** SOAR solutions will become more widely adopted to automate and orchestrate security incident response workflows.

The future of cloud security will be shaped by a combination of technological advancements, evolving threats, and changing business needs. Organizations that proactively adapt to these trends and invest in the right security solutions and skills will be best positioned to protect their data and applications in the cloud.

The Evolving Threat Landscape and Emerging Challenges

The cyber threat landscape is constantly evolving, becoming more sophisticated and complex. Several factors contribute to this evolution:

- **Increased Attack Surface:** The rapid adoption of cloud computing, IoT devices, and mobile technologies has dramatically expanded the attack surface. Attackers have more entry points to exploit.
- **Sophisticated Attack Techniques:** Attackers are using more advanced techniques, such as AI-powered phishing emails, polymorphic malware, and zero-day exploits.
- **Targeting Cloud Environments:** Cloud environments are becoming a prime target for attackers due to the vast amounts of data they store and the potential for large-scale breaches.
- **Rise of Ransomware:** Ransomware attacks are becoming more frequent and sophisticated, with attackers increasingly targeting cloud environments and demanding large ransoms.
- **Insider Threats:** Insider threats, whether malicious or accidental, continue to be a significant concern.
- **Geopolitical Conflicts:** Cyberattacks are increasingly being used as a tool in geopolitical conflicts, targeting critical infrastructure and government agencies.
- **Supply Chain Attacks:** Attackers are targeting software supply chains to introduce vulnerabilities into widely used applications.

The Rise of Serverless Computing and its Security Implications

Serverless computing (functions, FaaS) offers many advantages, but it also introduces unique security challenges:

- **Increased Attack Surface:** The distributed and ephemeral nature of serverless functions can make them more difficult to secure.
- **Code Vulnerabilities:** Serverless functions are often developed quickly, and security

may not be a primary focus, leading to vulnerabilities in the code.

- **Dependency Management:** Serverless functions rely on third-party libraries and dependencies, which can introduce security risks.
- **Access Control:** Properly managing access control for serverless functions is crucial, as misconfigurations can lead to unauthorized access.
- **Secrets Management:** Serverless functions often need to access sensitive information (API keys, passwords), and securely managing these secrets is essential.
- **Lack of Visibility:** Monitoring and securing serverless functions can be challenging due to their short lifespan and event-driven nature.
- **Cold Starts:** The latency associated with "cold starts" (when a function is invoked after a period of inactivity) can create timing windows that attackers might exploit.

The Impact of Quantum Computing on Cloud Security

Quantum computing has the potential to revolutionize many fields, but it also poses a significant threat to current encryption methods:

- **Breaking Current Encryption:** Quantum computers, when they become sufficiently powerful, will be able to break many of the widely used public-key encryption algorithms (like RSA) that currently secure our systems. This includes data at rest, data in transit, and digital signatures.
- **The Quantum Threat:** This poses a long-term threat to cloud security, as sensitive data stored today could be vulnerable to decryption by future quantum computers.
- **Transition to Quantum-Resistant Cryptography:** The cybersecurity community is actively working on developing quantum-resistant cryptography (also called post-quantum cryptography) to protect systems and data from future quantum attacks. This involves developing new cryptographic algorithms that are resistant to being broken by quantum computers.
- **Migration Challenges:** Migrating to quantum-resistant cryptography will be a complex and time-consuming process, as it will require updating many existing systems and protocols. Organizations need to start planning for this transition now.

Key Considerations for Addressing These Challenges:

- **Proactive Security:** Organizations need to adopt a more proactive approach to security, focusing on threat detection, prevention, and incident response.
- **Zero Trust Security:** Implementing a Zero Trust security model is crucial for protecting against evolving threats.
- **Security Automation:** Automating security tasks and incident response is essential for keeping pace with the rapid evolution of the threat landscape.
- **Cloud-Native Security:** Organizations need to adopt cloud-native security tools and practices to protect their cloud environments.
- **DevSecOps:** Integrating security into the DevOps pipeline is essential for building

secure applications and infrastructure.
- **Threat Intelligence:** Staying informed about the latest threats and vulnerabilities is crucial for proactively protecting against attacks.
- **Skills Development:** The cybersecurity industry needs to address the skills gap by training and developing cybersecurity professionals.
- **Quantum Readiness:** Organizations should begin planning for the transition to quantum-resistant cryptography to protect their data from future quantum computing attacks.

By understanding these evolving challenges and adopting appropriate security measures, organizations can better protect themselves from the increasingly sophisticated cyber threats they face. A layered and adaptive security approach is crucial for navigating the complex and dynamic world of cybersecurity.

The Importance of a Proactive and Integrated Approach to Cloud Security

Cloud security is not a one-time fix; it's an ongoing process. A *proactive* approach means anticipating threats, rather than simply reacting to incidents. An *integrated* approach means that all aspects of security work together seamlessly, rather than being isolated silos.

Why Proactive and Integrated Security is Essential:
- **Dynamic Cloud Environments:** Cloud environments are constantly changing, with new resources being provisioned and deprovisioned. A proactive approach allows you to keep pace with these changes and ensure security is maintained.
- **Evolving Threat Landscape:** The cyber threat landscape is constantly evolving, with new attacks and vulnerabilities emerging regularly. A proactive approach helps you stay ahead of these threats.
- **Complex Security Challenges:** Cloud security challenges are complex and require a multi-faceted approach. An integrated approach ensures that all aspects of security are considered and work together effectively.
- **Shared Responsibility Model:** Understanding the shared responsibility model between the cloud provider and the customer is crucial. A proactive approach helps you fulfill your responsibilities and ensure that your data and applications are protected.

Key Components of a Proactive and Integrated Approach:
- **Risk Management:** Identify and assess potential security risks. Prioritize risks based on their likelihood and impact.
- **Security Architecture:** Design a secure cloud architecture that incorporates security best practices and controls.
- **Security Controls:** Implement appropriate technical and administrative security

controls.

- **Security Monitoring and Logging:** Continuously monitor your cloud environment for security events and maintain detailed logs.
- **Threat Intelligence:** Stay informed about the latest threats and vulnerabilities.
- **Incident Response Planning:** Develop and regularly test incident response plans.
- **Security Awareness Training:** Educate employees about security best practices.
- **Vulnerability Management:** Regularly scan for vulnerabilities and apply patches.
- **Security Testing:** Conduct regular security testing, such as penetration testing and vulnerability assessments.

Continuous Monitoring, Assessment, and Improvement

This is the core of a proactive security approach.

- **Continuous Monitoring:** Use security tools and services to continuously monitor your cloud environment for security events, misconfigurations, and vulnerabilities. This includes monitoring network traffic, user activity, system logs, and security tool outputs.
- **Continuous Assessment:** Regularly assess your security posture using vulnerability scanners, penetration testing tools, and security audits. This helps you identify weaknesses and areas for improvement.
- **Continuous Improvement:** Based on the results of your monitoring and assessment, continuously improve your security controls and processes. This includes patching vulnerabilities, updating security configurations, and refining your security policies.

Building a Strong Security Culture within Organizations

Technology alone is not enough. A strong security culture is essential for effective cloud security. This means:

- **Leadership Commitment:** Security must be a priority for senior management.
- **Employee Awareness:** All employees should be aware of security risks and their responsibilities in protecting data and systems.
- **Security Training:** Provide regular security awareness training to all employees.
- **Clear Security Policies:** Establish clear and comprehensive security policies.
- **Incident Reporting:** Encourage employees to report security incidents.
- **Accountability:** Hold employees accountable for following security policies.
- **Open Communication:** Foster open communication about security issues.
- **Security Champions:** Identify and empower security champions within different departments.

How to Foster a Strong Security Culture

- **Make Security Relevant:** Explain why security is important and how it impacts employees' work.

- **Keep it Simple:** Make security policies and procedures easy to understand and follow.
- **Lead by Example:** Senior management should demonstrate their commitment to security.
- **Recognize and Reward:** Recognize and reward employees who follow security best practices.
- **Make it Fun:** Use gamification and other techniques to make security training more engaging.
- **Regular Communication:** Communicate regularly about security issues and best practices.

By implementing these principles and practices, organizations can build a robust and proactive cloud security program that protects their data and applications from evolving cyber threats. A strong security culture, combined with continuous monitoring, assessment, and improvement, is essential for long-term cloud security success.

Conclusion

Cloud computing offers tremendous benefits, but it also introduces a unique set of security challenges. Organizations must understand these challenges and implement appropriate solutions to protect their data and applications in the cloud.

In conclusion, cloud security is a shared responsibility and an ongoing journey. By adopting a proactive, integrated, and adaptive approach, organizations can effectively protect their data and applications in the cloud and navigate the evolving cyber threat landscape. It requires a commitment to continuous improvement, ongoing vigilance, and a strong security culture. The cloud offers incredible opportunities, but only with a robust and dynamic security posture can those opportunities be fully realized.

6

Cybersecurity Frameworks and Governance

The modern world is witnessing an exponential rise in cyber threats, ranging from sophisticated ransomware attacks to large-scale data breaches that compromise personal and corporate security. Organizations, governments, and individuals' increasing digital dependency has created a complex cybersecurity landscape in which traditional defense mechanisms often fall short. Without a structured and proactive strategy, organizations face the possibility of financial losses, reputational damage, and regulatory penalties. A well-defined cybersecurity framework and governance model are paramount for effectively navigating these challenges. Cybersecurity frameworks offer structured guidelines for assessing, mitigating, and responding to cyber threats, while governance strategies guarantee accountability, compliance, and ongoing improvement. By implementing robust frameworks such as NIST, ISO/IEC 27001, and GDPR, organisations can create a strong foundation for risk management and security resilience. Moreover, promoting a culture of security within an organisation is crucial.

Cybersecurity is not merely the responsibility of IT departments; rather, it requires an integrated approach that involves leadership, employees, and stakeholders. This chapter explores the importance of cybersecurity frameworks, governance models, and security culture, illustrating how organisations can strengthen their defences against an evolving threat landscape.

Global Cybersecurity Frameworks

Cybersecurity frameworks provide a comprehensive and systematic approach to protecting digital assets against an increasingly diverse array of cyber threats. These frameworks establish a foundational structure through which organisations can methodically evaluate risks, implement stringent security controls, and cultivate long-term resilience against adversarial incursions. A well-executed framework not only enhances an organisation's capacity to prevent cyber incidents but also ensures the existence of effective incident response and recovery protocols. By understanding and utilising global frameworks, organisations can align their security strategies with established best practices and regulatory mandates, thereby reinforcing a proactive cyber defence posture. The subsequent sections present a thorough examination of essential global frameworks that influence contemporary cybersecurity practices.

NIST Cybersecurity Framework (CSF)

The National Institute of Standards and Technology (NIST) Cybersecurity Framework (CSF) is one of the most widely adopted cybersecurity frameworks globally, providing a risk-based approach to managing cybersecurity threats. Developed by NIST, the CSF aims to help organisations of all sizes and sectors enhance cybersecurity resilience through a systematic and scalable framework methodology.

The framework is built around five core functions, each of which represents a critical aspect of cybersecurity management:

- **Identify**: Organizations must develop a deep understanding of their cybersecurity risks by identifying critical assets, assessing vulnerabilities, and determining potential threats. This function involves asset management, business environment analysis, governance, risk assessment, and supply chain risk management.
- **Protect**: This function focuses on implementing safeguards to ensure the delivery of essential services. Protection measures include identity and access management, awareness training, data security controls, protective technology, and maintenance strategies to defend against cyber threats.
- **Detect**: Organizations need to establish processes for continuous monitoring and anomaly detection. This includes implementing security monitoring systems, detection processes, and event analysis tools such as Security Information and Event Management (SIEM) and intrusion detection systems (IDS).
- **Respond**: A well-structured response plan is essential in a cybersecurity incident. This function encompasses incident response planning, communications, mitigation techniques, and improvements based on past incidents.
- **Recover**: Organizations must develop strategies to restore normal operations after a security breach. The recovery process includes resilience planning, business continuity strategies, and system restoration activities to minimise the long-term impact of cyber incidents.

Implementation Tiers

The NIST Cybersecurity Framework (CSF) introduces implementation tiers to help organisations assess the maturity of their cybersecurity practices. These tiers range from Partial (Tier 1) to Adaptive (Tier 4), with increasing levels of integration, risk management, and governance alignment:

- **Tier 1 (Partial):** Organizations at this level have limited cybersecurity awareness and unstructured risk management practices.
- **Tier 2 (Risk-Informed):** Organizations develop some risk management practices but lack a formalised cybersecurity program.
- **Tier 3 (Repeatable):** Cybersecurity policies and risk management strategies are well-established and consistently applied across the organisation.
- **Tier 4 (Adaptive):** Organizations integrate real-time threat intelligence, continuously evolve their cybersecurity strategies, and proactively manage emerging risks.

Profiles and Customization

A significant strength of the NIST Cybersecurity Framework (CSF) is its inherent flexibility. Organisations have the opportunity to develop profiles that align with their unique security requirements, industry regulations, and operational objectives. These profiles enable the customisation of the framework to address specific needs, thereby ensuring a tailored approach to security management cybersecurity.

Benefits of Adopting NIST CSF

Organisations that adopt the NIST Cybersecurity Framework benefit from:

- A standardised approach to risk management and cybersecurity governance.
- Enhanced resilience against evolving cyber threats.
- Improved compliance with industry regulations and international security standards.
- Better communication between technical teams and executive leadership by aligning security with business objectives.
- Scalability and adaptability make it suitable for organizations of all sizes.

By adhering to the NIST Cybersecurity Framework (CSF), organisations can establish a robust cybersecurity foundation that helps them anticipate, prevent, and respond to cyber threats effectively.

ISO/IEC 27001

ISO/IEC 27001 is an internationally recognised standard that systematically manages sensitive corporate information and protects its integrity. It outlines the criteria for an Information Security Management System (ISMS) and is specifically designed to help organisations establish, implement, maintain, and continuously enhance their information security protocols practices.

Key Components of ISO/IEC 27001

ISO/IEC 27001 is structured around a process-based approach to risk management and includes several core components:

- Information Security Management System (ISMS): The central framework that outlines policies, procedures, and controls to manage information security risks.
- Risk Assessment and Treatment: Organizations must conduct risk assessments to identify vulnerabilities and implement appropriate security measures to mitigate identified risks.
- Leadership Commitment: Executive leadership is crucial in enforcing security policies and ensuring continuous compliance.
- Context of the Organization: Companies must define the internal and external factors that affect their information security risks.
- Security Controls: The standard provides a set of security controls covering access control, cryptography, operations security, incident management, and more.

ISO/IEC 27001 Certification Process

Achieving ISO/IEC 27001 certification involves several steps:

- Gap Analysis: Organizations assess their security posture against ISO/IEC 27001 requirements.
- Implementing ISMS: Developing policies, security controls, and processes to align with the standard.
- Internal Audit: Conducting internal reviews ensures all security measures are effectively implemented.
- Certification Audit: A formal assessment by an accredited certification body to validate compliance with the standard.
- Continuous Improvement: Regular monitoring and updates to enhance security measures and address emerging threats.

Benefits of ISO/IEC 27001 Compliance

Adopting ISO/IEC 27001 provides multiple advantages for organisations:

- Enhanced Security Posture: A structured approach to managing security threats and protecting sensitive data.
- Regulatory Compliance: Helps organisations meet legal and regulatory requirements related to data protection.
- Risk Mitigation: Proactively identifying and mitigating security risks reduces the likelihood of breaches.
- Improved Customer Trust: Certification demonstrates a commitment to security and promotes trust among clients and partners.
- Operational Efficiency: Streamlined security processes enhance business operations and resilience.

Implementing ISO/IEC 27001 can help organisations establish a strong framework for managing cybersecurity risks, ensuring business continuity, and demonstrating regulatory compliance.

CIS Controls

The Centre for Internet Security (CIS) Controls provides a comprehensive set of best practices to strengthen organisations against prevalent cyber threats. These controls establish a practical security framework organisations can implement to enhance their cybersecurity posture. The CIS Controls are remarkably esteemed for their effectiveness in minimising attack surfaces and enhancing defensive measures capabilities.

Structure of CIS Controls

CIS Controls are categorised into three distinct implementation groups, allowing organisations to prioritise security measures based on their resources and risk appetite:

- **Basic Controls (IG1)**: These fundamental security measures establish essential cybersecurity hygiene, including inventory management, secure configurations, and continuous vulnerability management.
- **Foundational Controls (IG2)**: Intermediate measures that strengthen cybersecurity defences, such as managing administrative privileges, email security configurations, and monitoring network activity.
- **Organisational Controls (IG3)**: Advanced security strategies tailored for large enterprises, including penetration testing, red team exercises, security awareness training, and incident response management.

Key CIS Controls

The CIS framework comprises 18 key controls that help organisations address various security risks. Some of the most critical controls include:

- Inventory and Control of Enterprise Assets: Maintaining an accurate inventory of all hardware and software assets to prevent unauthorised access.
- Secure Configuration of Enterprise Assets and Software: Ensuring that operating systems and applications are configured with strong security settings to mitigate vulnerabilities.
- Data Protection: Implementing encryption, access control policies, and data loss prevention strategies to safeguard sensitive information.
- Continuous Vulnerability Management: Regularly scanning for vulnerabilities and applying patches to eliminate potential security threats.
- Controlled Use of Administrative Privileges: This method restricts administrative access to only necessary personnel, reducing the risk of privilege escalation attacks.
- Audit Log Management: Maintaining comprehensive logs of security-related events to enable forensic investigations and compliance monitoring.
- Email and Web Browser Protections: Deploy security controls to filter malicious emails,

block phishing attempts, and enforce safe browsing practices.

- Malware Defenses: Implementing advanced threat detection and response mechanisms to identify and neutralise malware threats.
- Security Awareness and Skills Training: Educating employees on cybersecurity best practices to reduce human-related security risks.
- Incident Response and Management: Establishing an incident response plan to swiftly contain, mitigate, and recover from security breaches.

Benefits of Implementing CIS Controls

Organisations that adopt CIS Controls can experience several benefits, including:

- Improved Cyber Resilience: Strengthens an organisation's ability to effectively detect, prevent, and respond to cyber threats.
- Regulatory Compliance: Aligns with industry regulations such as GDPR, HIPAA, and PCI DSS, facilitating easier compliance.
- Reduced Attack Surface: Minimizes the risk of cyberattacks by implementing essential security measures.
- Cost-Effective Security Enhancements: Provides a prioritised approach that enables organisations to implement controls based on available resources and threat exposure.
- Proven Industry Standards: CIS Controls are widely recognised by cybersecurity professionals and government agencies as effective defence mechanisms.

By incorporating CIS Controls into their cybersecurity strategy, organisations can establish a systematic and proactive methodology for mitigating cyber threats and ensuring a resilient security environment.

COBIT (Control Objectives for Information and Related Technologies)

COBIT is an IT governance and management framework that provides a structured approach to aligning IT and cybersecurity strategies with business objectives. Developed by ISACA, COBIT ensures that IT systems are effectively governed, risks are managed, and regulatory compliance is maintained.

Core Principles of COBIT

COBIT is built upon five key principles:

- Meeting Stakeholder Needs: Ensures business objectives align with IT and security strategies to maximise value.
- Covering the Enterprise End-to-End: Provides governance across the entire organisation rather than focusing solely on IT.
- Applying a Single Integrated Framework: COBIT integrates various standards and regulations, such as ISO 27001, NIST, and ITIL, into a cohesive approach.

- Enabling a Holistic Approach: Covers multiple governance components, including processes, structures, and information flow.
- Separating Governance from Management: This clearly defines the roles and responsibilities of governance (setting policies and direction) and management (executing policies and practices).

COBIT Framework Structure

COBIT comprises various components that guide organisations in implementing effective governance:

- Governance and Management Objectives: Organized into five domains: Evaluate, Direct, and Monitor (EDM); Align, Plan, and Organize (APO); Build, Acquire, and Implement (BAI); Deliver, Service, and Support (DSS); and Monitor, Evaluate, and Assess (MEA).
- Processes: These include structured processes that support IT governance and risk management.
- Performance Metrics: Establishes Key Performance Indicators (KPIs) and Key Risk Indicators (KRIs) to measure cybersecurity effectiveness.

COBIT Implementation Benefits

Organisations that implement COBIT can achieve:

- Stronger IT and Business Alignment: Enhancing decision-making by integrating IT and cybersecurity into overall business goals.
- Improved Risk Management: Identifying, assessing, and mitigating cybersecurity risks through structured policies and controls.
- Regulatory Compliance: Ensuring adherence to industry regulations and best practices for data protection and security.
- Efficient IT Resource Utilization: Optimizing IT investments and ensuring cost-effective cybersecurity implementations.
- Enhanced Security Governance: Establishing accountability and a clear division between governance and operational security responsibilities.

COBIT in Cybersecurity Governance

COBIT provides an essential foundation for establishing cybersecurity governance by defining:

- Risk management policies and controls.
- Security investment strategies that align with business objectives.
- Compliance monitoring and continuous improvement mechanisms.

By utilising COBIT, organisations can incorporate security governance into enterprise-wide strategies, ensuring resilience against evolving cyber threats while maintaining compliance and operational integrity efficiency.

PCI DSS (Payment Card Industry Data Security Standard)

The Payment Card Industry Data Security Standard (PCI DSS) is a globally recognized framework designed to protect cardholder data and ensuring secure payment transactions. This standard has been developed by the Payment Card Industry Security Standards Council (PCI SSC) and is applicable to all entities engaged in the processing, storage, or transmission of credit card information, including but not limited to merchants, payment processors, and financial institutions.

Key Requirements of PCI DSS

PCI DSS consists of 12 core security requirements grouped into six broad objectives:

1. Build and Maintain a Secure Network and Systems
    - Install and maintain firewalls to protect cardholder data.
    - Avoid using vendor-supplied default passwords and security configurations.
2. Protect Cardholder Data
    - Encrypt stored cardholder data.
    - Implement strong cryptographic measures to secure the transmission of cardholder data across public networks.
3. Maintain a Vulnerability Management Program
    - Use and regularly update antivirus software.
    - Develop and maintain secure applications and systems.
4. Implement Strong Access Control Measures
    - Restrict access to cardholder data to authorised personnel only.
    - Assign unique IDs to individuals with computer access.
    - Restrict physical access to cardholder data storage facilities.
5. Regularly Monitor and Test Networks
    - Track and monitor all access to network resources and cardholder data.
    - Conduct regular security testing and vulnerability assessments.
6. Maintain an Information Security Policy
    - Establish, publish, and maintain an organisational security policy.
    - Conduct security awareness training for employees.

Compliance and Validation Requirements

Depending on their transaction volume and risk profile, organisations subject to PCI DSS must regularly validate compliance through audits, self-assessments, and third-party assessments. The four levels of PCI DSS compliance are:

- **Level 1:** Merchants processing over 6 million transactions annually (requires an external audit and penetration testing).

- **Level 2:** Merchants processing between 1 and 6 million transactions annually (requires self-assessment and vulnerability scanning).
- **Level 3:** Merchants processing between 20,000 and 1 million transactions annually (self-assessment required).
- **Level 4:** Merchants processing fewer than 20,000 transactions annually (requires periodic security reviews).

Benefits of PCI DSS Compliance

Organisations that comply with PCI DSS can experience several advantages, including:

- **Enhanced Data Security:** Reduces the risk of data breaches and fraud by enforcing stringent security measures.
- **Regulatory Compliance:** Helps meet legal and industry requirements related to payment security.
- **Improved Customer Trust:** Enhances brand reputation by demonstrating a commitment to safeguarding financial information.
- **Lower Financial Risks:** Avoids non-compliance penalties and potential liability associated with data breaches.
- **Stronger Incident Response Readiness:** Establishes structured protocols for detecting, mitigating, and responding to security incidents.

Challenges in PCI DSS Implementation

While PCI DSS enhances payment security, organisations often face challenges in compliance, such as:

- **The complexity of Implementation:** Meeting all 12 security requirements can be resource-intensive.
- **Evolving Threat Landscape:** Cybercriminals continually develop new attack vectors, requiring constant security updates.
- **Ongoing Maintenance:** PCI DSS compliance is not a one-time task but requires continuous monitoring, testing, and updates.

By adhering to PCI DSS, organisations handling payment transactions can strengthen their security infrastructure, protect customer payment data, and mitigate the risks associated with cyber threats in the financial sector.

GDPR (General Data Protection Regulation)

The General Data Protection Regulation (GDPR) is a comprehensive data privacy law enacted by the European Union to protect the personal data of EU citizens. The GDPR aims to enhance individuals' control over personal information and establish clear guidelines for organisations handling such data. Compliance with the GDPR is not limited to EU-based companies; it applies to any organisation worldwide that collects, processes, or stores the data of EU citizens.

Core Principles of GDPR

GDPR is founded on several key principles that dictate how personal data should be handled:

- Lawfulness, Fairness, and Transparency: Data must be processed lawfully, fairly, and transparently.
- Purpose Limitation: Data should be collected for specified, explicit, and legitimate purposes and not used beyond those.
- Data Minimization: Organizations should only collect the necessary data for a specific purpose.
- Accuracy: Data must be kept accurate and up to date, with processes in place to correct inaccuracies.
- Storage Limitation: Personal data should not be retained longer than necessary for the intended purpose.
- Integrity and Confidentiality: Organizations must protect personal data against unauthorised or unlawful processing, accidental loss, destruction, or damage.
- Accountability: Organizations must be able to demonstrate compliance with these principles.

Key Rights of Individuals under GDPR

GDPR grants individuals significant rights over their data, including:

- Right to Access: Individuals can request access to their data and understand how it is used.
- Right to Rectification: Users can request corrections to inaccurate or incomplete data.
- Right to Erasure (Right to be Forgotten): Individuals can request deletion of their data under specific conditions.
- Right to Restrict Processing: Users can limit how their data is processed.
- Right to Data Portability: Individuals can receive their data in a structured, commonly used format and transfer it to another organisation.
- Right to Object: Individuals can object to data processing, particularly in direct marketing scenarios.
- Rights Related to Automated Decision Making and Profiling: Individuals can opt out of automated decision-making, including profiling.

Compliance Requirements for Organizations

Organisations must take specific measures to comply with GDPR, including:

- Obtaining Explicit Consent: Data collection must be based on clear and affirmative user consent.
- Data Protection by Design and Default: Organizations must integrate data protection into systems and processes from the outset.
- Appointing a Data Protection Officer (DPO): Large-scale data processors must appoint a DPO to oversee compliance.
- Conducting Data Protection Impact Assessments (DPIAs): Organizations must evaluate risks associated with processing personal data.
- Implementing Security Measures: Strong encryption, pseudonymisation, and access controls should be employed to protect data.
- Breach Notification Requirements: Organizations must report data breaches to authorities within 72 hours and inform affected individuals when necessary.

Penalties for Non-Compliance

Non-compliance with GDPR can result in severe financial penalties. Additionally, reputational damage and loss of customer trust can significantly impact business operations.
Benefits of GDPR Compliance
While GDPR imposes strict regulations, compliance brings several advantages:

- Enhanced Data Security: Strengthens cybersecurity measures and reduces the risk of breaches.
- Improved Customer Trust: Demonstrates commitment to privacy and data protection.
- Regulatory Alignment: Helps organisations align with other data protection laws globally.
- Competitive Advantage: GDPR compliance can differentiate businesses as trustworthy and security-conscious.

GDPR has established a global benchmark for data privacy laws, influencing other regulations such as the California Consumer Privacy Act (CCPA) and Brazil's General Data Protection Law (LGPD). By adhering to GDPR, organisations can ensure robust data protection, promote customer trust, and avoid costly repercussions and penalties.

Governance Strategies

Effective cybersecurity governance forms the foundation of an organisation's ability to mitigate cyber threats, ensure compliance with regulatory requirements, and maintain operational resilience. Governance strategies not only establish accountability but also create a structured framework for decision-making, risk management, and incident response. A well-implemented governance model promotes a culture of security and integrates cybersecurity considerations into business operations across all levels.

Cybersecurity governance is a dynamic process that evolves alongside emerging threats, technological advancements, and changing regulatory landscapes. Organisations must establish governance strategies that are flexible, scalable, and enforceable across all departments. The following sections examine the core governance strategies organisations must implement to enhance their cybersecurity posture.

Risk Management Frameworks

Risk management frameworks function as a structured methodology for identifying, assessing, mitigating, and monitoring cybersecurity risks within an organisation. They establish a systematic approach for managing uncertainties and minimising the potential impact of cyber threats. By implementing a practical risk management framework, organisations can proactively address security vulnerabilities, safeguard critical assets, and ensure business continuity during cyber incidents.

One of the fundamental aspects of a risk management framework is risk assessment, which involves identifying assets, evaluating potential threats, and determining the vulnerabilities that malicious actors could exploit. This process includes understanding the probability of occurrence and potential impact of each risk, enabling organisations to prioritise mitigation strategies effectively. Depending on their operational requirements and industry regulations, organisations may use quantitative or qualitative risk assessment models.

Upon identifying risks, the subsequent step pertains to risk mitigation and treatment. Organisations may select from four primary risk management strategies: risk avoidance, risk reduction, risk transfer, and risk acceptance. Risk avoidance entails eliminating activities that expose the organisation to potential threats. Risk reduction involves the implementation of security controls such as firewalls, intrusion detection systems, and encryption to minimise vulnerabilities. Risk transfer consists of shifting the financial burden associated with potential cyber incidents to a third party, such as a provider of cybersecurity insurance. Risk acceptance occurs when an organisation acknowledges a risk but considers it manageable or insignificant in cost versus potential impact benefit.

A robust risk management framework also incorporates continuous monitoring and evaluation to address evolving cyber threats dynamically. Systematic security assessments, penetration testing, and vulnerability scanning are instrumental in enabling organizations to respond to emerging risks effectively. Furthermore, governance mechanisms, including compliance audits and incident response evaluations, significantly enhance the efficacy of risk management practices strategies.

Several widely recognised risk management frameworks guide organisations in implementing best practices. These include:

- NIST Risk Management Framework (RMF): Developed by the National Institute of

Standards and Technology, RMF provides a structured, multi-tiered approach to integrating risk management into the system development life cycle.

- ISO 31000: This international standard provides principles and guidelines for effective risk management applicable across various industries.
- FAIR (Factor Analysis of Information Risk): A quantitative risk assessment framework that enables organisations to evaluate financial exposure due to cybersecurity threats.

By utilizing these frameworks, organizations can establish a resilient risk management strategy that aligns with business objectives, regulatory requirements, and industry best practices. This proactive approach ensures the effective management of cybersecurity risks, thereby diminishing the likelihood of financial losses, reputational damage, and operational..

Security Policies and Procedures

Security policies and procedures form the foundation of an organisation's cybersecurity governance framework. These policies outline clear directives regarding security maintenance, ensuring consistency across all departments and reducing vulnerabilities that may be exploited by malicious actors. Furthermore, effective security policies support a systematic approach to risk management, guarantee compliance with regulatory requirements, and promote a culture focused on security awareness.

A well-defined security policy should outline acceptable use policies, governing how employees and third parties access and use organisational systems. This includes rules regarding password management, internet usage, email security, and device management to prevent unauthorised access and data breaches. Furthermore, organisations must implement data classification and handling procedures that specify how sensitive information is stored, transmitted, and disposed of to mitigate risks associated with data leaks and unauthorised access exposure.

Incident response and reporting mechanisms are essential elements of security policies. Organisations must establish clear protocols for detecting, responding to, and mitigating security incidents. This involves forming an incident response team, defining roles and responsibilities, and outlining escalation procedures. Ensuring that employees understand and adhere to these protocols enhances the organisation's ability to respond swiftly to cyber threats, thereby minimising potential risks damages.

Regular policy reviews and updates are imperative to adapt to the continuously evolving cybersecurity landscape. Organizations ought to undertake periodic security audits and compliance assessments to identify any deficiencies in policies and implement the required modifications. Moreover, security awareness training programs should be seamlessly incorporated into governance strategies, ensuring that all employees are comprehensively informed about security policies and their responsibilities in upholding cybersecurity resilience.

Implementing robust security policies and procedures can help organisations take a structured and proactive approach to managing cybersecurity risks. This ensures regulatory compliance and strengthens the overall security posture, making it harder for cyber threats to disrupt business operations.

Compliance and Regulatory Adherence

Compliance and regulatory adherence are crucial components of cybersecurity governance. They ensure that organisations meet legal and industry requirements to protect sensitive data and maintain security standards. Regulatory frameworks provide structured guidelines organisations must follow to mitigate risks, prevent data breaches, and uphold customer trust. With the rise in cyber threats and stringent data protection laws, compliance is not merely a legal necessity but also a strategic imperative.

Organisations must adhere to various industry regulations, such as GDPR (General Data Protection Regulation), HIPAA (Health Insurance Portability and Accountability Act), and CCPA (California Consumer Privacy Act). These regulations establish legal frameworks for data protection, emphasising transparency, accountability, and user rights. Failure to comply with these laws can result in substantial fines, legal consequences, and reputational damage. To achieve regulatory compliance, organisations should establish a compliance management programme that incorporates regular risk assessments, policy enforcement, and ongoing monitoring. An essential element of compliance is performing regular audits and gap analyses to identify vulnerabilities and ensure that security measures are aligned with evolving regulations. Audits enable organisations to proactively address deficiencies, update security policies, and strengthen cybersecurity governance.

Furthermore, organisations should adopt compliance automation tools to enhance regulatory processes. These tools help in monitoring compliance status, tracking policy updates, and generating reports for regulatory bodies. Implementing encryption, access controls, and data classification mechanisms also plays a crucial role in achieving compliance standards.

Ultimately, maintaining compliance is an ongoing process that demands adaptability to changing regulations and cybersecurity threats. Organisations must remain informed about legislative changes, invest in employee training programmes, and enforce security protocols to meet regulatory requirements. By prioritising compliance, organisations can enhance cybersecurity resilience, protect sensitive information, and demonstrate commitment to ethical and legal responsibilities in the digital landscape.

Incident Response and Recovery Planning

Incident response and recovery planning are essential components of cybersecurity governance, ensuring that organisations can proficiently manage and mitigate cyber threats. A meticulously defined incident response plan minimises the impact of security incidents, expedites the restoration of operations, and helps prevent future occurrences. Without a structured approach, organisations expose themselves to the risks of extended downtime, financial losses, and reputational damage.

A comprehensive incident response strategy comprises several essential components phases:

- **Preparation**: Organizations must develop policies, tools, and training programs to ensure readiness during a cyber incident. This includes defining roles and responsibilities, establishing an incident response team, and conducting regular cybersecurity drills.
- **Detection and Analysis**: To limit damage, it is crucial to identify security breaches in real time. This phase involves continuously monitoring networks, analysing alerts from intrusion detection systems, and utilising threat intelligence to recognise anomalies.
- **Containment, Eradication, and Recovery**: Once an incident is identified, immediate containment measures must be taken to prevent further damage. This includes isolating affected systems, removing malicious software, and implementing patches or security updates. The recovery process involves restoring normal operations, validating system integrity, and ensuring no residual vulnerabilities remain.
- **Post-Incident Review and Improvement**: After handling an incident, organisations should conduct a thorough review to analyse the root cause, assess the effectiveness of their response, and update security protocols accordingly. Lessons learned from each incident should be documented and incorporated into future planning to enhance resilience.

Organisations should also implement communication strategies to support effective incident response and ensure timely reporting to stakeholders, regulatory bodies, and affected individuals when required. A well-coordinated response minimises disruptions and reinforces trust and compliance with legal obligations. By integrating incident response and recovery planning into cybersecurity governance, organisations can build a proactive security posture, enhance resilience, and mitigate the consequences of evolving cyber threats.

Security Awareness and Training

Security awareness and training are essential components of an organisation's cybersecurity strategy. They ensure that employees and stakeholders understand security risks and follow best practices to protect digital assets. As human error remains one of the leading causes of cyber incidents, an effective training program helps mitigate threats such as phishing attacks, social engineering, and weak authentication practices.

A comprehensive security awareness program should educate employees at all levels about the evolving nature of cyber threats. Training should cover password hygiene, secure browsing habits, the dangers of unsecured public Wi-Fi, and how to identify malicious emails. Interactive learning techniques, including simulated phishing attacks and real-world cyber incident case studies, reinforce learning and enhance retention.

Organisations should implement a structured training programme that includes periodic refresher courses, role-specific training for different departments, and mandatory cybersecurity awareness sessions for new recruits. Advanced training for IT and security teams should concentrate on incident response, secure software development, and emerging threats such as AI-driven cyberattacks and deepfakes technology.

Organisations must incorporate security awareness into their routine operations to cultivate a culture of cybersecurity vigilance. Regular security drills, gamified educational methodologies, and positive reinforcement strategies, such as rewarding employees for reporting suspicious activities, enhance engagement and accountability. Furthermore, leadership should exemplify commitment by prioritising cybersecurity best practices and actively participating in training initiatives.

Security awareness and training programmes must be consistently updated to align with the latest threats, regulatory changes, and technological advancements. Regular assessments, including quizzes and simulations, provide measurable insights into employee preparedness and help identify areas requiring attention improvement. By cultivating a culture of security awareness, organisations can significantly reduce the risk of cyber incidents, strengthen their overall security posture, and ensure that employees become an active line of defence against cyber threats.

Building a Culture of Security

Establishing a robust security culture is a fundamental aspect of an organisation's overall cybersecurity strategy. It transcends technical defences and policy enforcement, embedding security awareness into the mindset and daily operations of all employees. Cybersecurity is no longer solely the responsibility of IT teams; rather, it requires the active participation of leadership, employees, and stakeholders at all levels. Organisations that cultivate a strong security culture significantly mitigate risks associated with human error, social engineering, and insider threats.

The foundation of a security culture begins with executive leadership. Senior management must lead by example and show a commitment to security by prioritising investments in cybersecurity infrastructure, integrating security into business strategies, and regularly communicating the importance of data protection. Leadership must also establish clear security policies and ensure compliance with industry standards, reinforcing that security is a collective effort responsibility.

Employee engagement and awareness play crucial roles in enhancing a security-conscious environment. Organisations must provide ongoing security training tailored to different roles within the company. Basic training should cover topics such as recognising phishing attacks, using strong passwords, securing personal devices, and reporting suspicious activity. Advanced training for IT and security professionals should address threat hunting, secure coding, and incident response strategies. Implementing gamified learning experiences, simulated cyberattacks, and real-world case studies enhances employee participation and retention of security best practices. It is essential to create an atmosphere where employees feel empowered to report security incidents . Organizations should establish clear, accessible, and anonymous reporting mechanisms for security concerns, potential breaches, or suspicious activities. Encouraging a non-punitive approach to reporting errors helps cultivate an open and proactive security culture. Integrating security into business processes is another key factor in strengthening an organisation's cybersecurity posture.

Cybersecurity should be embedded in the software development lifecycle (SDLC), supply chain management, and risk assessment procedures. Practices such as DevSecOps, which incorporate security into development from the outset, assist organisations in proactively addressing security vulnerabilities. Regular security audits, risk assessments, and compliance checks ensure continuous improvement and adaptation to emerging threats. Organisations should conduct penetration testing, security drills, and tabletop exercises to evaluate their preparedness and refine response strategies. Furthermore, promoting cross-departmental collaboration between security teams, human resources, and compliance officers ensures that cybersecurity efforts are comprehensive and practical across all operational areas.

Ultimately, a robust security culture transforms employees from the weakest link in cybersecurity into an organisation's first line of defence. By prioritising leadership engagement, ongoing training, risk-aware business processes, and proactive incident reporting, organisations can cultivate a resilient security culture that significantly diminishes the likelihood of cyber incidents and strengthens their overall security posture.

Conclusion

The evolving cybersecurity landscape demands a structured and comprehensive approach to managing threats, risks, and compliance requirements. Cybersecurity frameworks and governance models provide organisations with the essential tools and strategies to enhance their security posture, safeguard critical assets, and ensure regulatory compliance. By adopting globally recognised frameworks such as NIST CSF, ISO/IEC 27001, CIS Controls, COBIT, PCI DSS, and GDPR, organisations can implement standardised security measures that mitigate risks and enhance overall resilience. These frameworks establish best practices for cybersecurity and facilitate alignment between security and business objectives, ensuring that security initiatives support long-term organisations. Governance strategies are essential for embedding cybersecurity within an organisation's framework. Effective risk management frameworks enable organisations to proactively identify, assess, and address security threats. Security policies and procedures establish a consistent and enforceable security culture, while compliance with regulations guarantees legal and ethical data protection practices. Incident response and recovery planning prepare organisations to swiftly mitigate and recover from security incidents, thereby reducing operational disruptions. Furthermore, ongoing security awareness and training programmes cultivate a culture in which employees actively participate in an organisation's cybersecurity efforts defense.

A strong culture of security is vital for cultivating a proactive cybersecurity mindset. It necessitates commitment from leadership, engagement from employees, seamless integrationf security into business processes, and continuous assessment of security practices. Organisations that prioritise a security-first culture empower their workforce, reduce human-related vulnerabilities, and enhance their overall cyber resilience. As cyber threats evolve, organisations must remain vigilant, adaptable, and committed to continuous improvement. Regular updates to security frameworks, governance policies, and awareness initiatives are essential to ensure that cybersecurity measures remain effective against emerging threats. By promoting collaboration across departments, investing in advanced security technologies, and staying informed about regulatory changes, organisations can maintain robust and future-ready cybersecurity posture. Cybersecurity is not a one-off initiative but an ongoing commitment to safeguarding digital assets and maintaining trust in an interconnected world. By enhancing the principles discussed in this chapter, organisations can create a secure and resilient digital environment, protecting both their operations and stakeholders from the ever-increasing threat landscape.

7

Real-World Case Studies

Studying real-world cybersecurity incidents provides organisations with critical insights to strengthen their security posture and governance strategies. These cases highlight how threats evolve and demonstrate practical approaches to risk management, incident response, and compliance.

Cybersecurity Governance: The Role of Leadership

Effective cybersecurity governance forms the backbone of an organisation's security strategy. Leadership plays a vital role in driving initiatives, enforcing compliance, and fostering a culture of security awareness. Superficial policies are insufficient; true governance requires:

- **Continuous investment** in security frameworks
- Robust risk management strategies
- Alignment of security objectives with business goals

Example: Equifax Data Breach (2017)

In this breach, an unpatched Apache Struts vulnerability led to the exposure of personal data for 147 million individuals. The incident highlighted governance failures in risk management and vulnerability mitigation. Key takeaways include:

- Conduct regular security audits and risk assessments
- Comply with standards such as **ISO/IEC 27001** for systematic risk management
- Implement mandatory security awareness training to reduce human error risks
- Develop comprehensive incident response plans with clear reporting lines

Leadership accountability is crucial. Executives must prioritise cybersecurity investments aligned with organisational goals to strengthen overall resilience.

Preparing for the Quantum Computing Threat

Quantum computing promises unprecedented processing power but poses significant risks to current encryption standards such as RSA and ECC. A pressing concern is **"harvest now, decrypt later" attacks**, where data is collected today in anticipation of future quantum decryption capabilities.

Example: U.S. Government's Post-Quantum Cryptography Initiative

The **National Institute of Standards and Technology (NIST)** is developing quantum-resistant cryptographic standards to protect data against future quantum attacks. Key strategies for organisations include:

- Assess current cryptographic dependencies to identify vulnerable assets
- Transition to **Post-Quantum Cryptography (PQC)** using hybrid models that combine traditional and quantum-resistant algorithms
- Update governance frameworks and security policies to include post-quantum strategies
- Collaborate with industry groups and government initiatives to stay updated on evolving standards
- Invest in technologies like **Quantum Key Distribution (QKD)** for theoretically unbreakable encryption

Preparing now will safeguard sensitive data against future quantum-enabled threats.

Implementing Holistic Security Frameworks for Defence

Fragmented cybersecurity approaches expose organisations to persistent threats. Adopting comprehensive frameworks integrates security into risk management, compliance, incident response, and organisational culture.

Examples of Effective Frameworks

- NIST Cybersecurity Framework (CSF)
- Zero Trust Architecture (ZTA)
- ISO/IEC 27001

Key principles include

- **Continuous monitoring and adaptive policies** to detect and respond to threats efficiently

- **Zero Trust** – never implicitly trust; always verify users and devices
- **Risk-based decision-making** to allocate resources effectively and align security investments with business priorities

Example: NIST CSF Implementation in a Financial Institution

After a phishing attack compromised sensitive financial data, a global bank implemented the NIST CSF. Actions included:

- Real-time monitoring and behavioural analytics for early anomaly detection
- Regular penetration tests and vulnerability assessments to identify security gaps
- Comprehensive incident response planning to minimise downtime and losses
- Strict identity verification and access controls to reduce insider threats

This holistic approach fostered cross-team collaboration and embedded security into daily operations, enhancing resilience against emerging threats.

Conclusion

In this chapter, we learned:

- **Leadership commitment and governance** are fundamental to cybersecurity success
- **Quantum computing threats** require proactive preparation through PQC and QKD strategies
- **Holistic security frameworks** such as NIST CSF and Zero Trust Architecture build resilient organisational defences.

8

Future Directions in Cybersecurity

The rapid acceleration of digital transformation has fundamentally reshaped the cybersecurity landscape, introducing new complexities, threats, and opportunities. As organisations, governments, and individuals increasingly integrate emerging technologies into everyday operations, they encounter an ever-expanding attack surface that requires innovative security solutions. Traditional defence mechanisms are no longer sufficient to combat sophisticated cyber threats, now powered by artificial intelligence, quantum computing, and advanced automation. Furthermore, the rise of ransomware campaigns, supply chain vulnerabilities, and geopolitical cyber warfare has made cybersecurity a critical priority for enterprise nations.

To stay ahead, cybersecurity professionals must implement forward-thinking strategies that anticipate future trends and proactively address emerging threats rather than merely responding to them as they occur. Predictive analytics, machine learning-driven threat intelligence, and decentralised security architectures will significantly influence cybersecurity. Cutting-edge technologies, including blockchain for data integrity and quantum-safe cryptography, will transform our approach to cybersecurity. Concurrently, escalating threats such as deepfake-based fraud and AI-enhanced attacks will substantially challenge existing defence mechanisms.

This chapter explores the essential components of the future cybersecurity landscape, including predictive analytics, emerging technologies, and the evolving threat ecosystem. By comprehensively understanding these elements, organisations can shift from reactive cybersecurity measures to proactive, intelligence-driven security strategies.

Predictive Analytics and Cybersecurity

The emergence of sophisticated cyber threats necessitates a proactive approach to cybersecurity, shifting from reactive defence mechanisms to predictive threat detection.

Predictive analytics, empowered by artificial intelligence (AI) and machine learning (ML), is revolutionising cybersecurity by allowing organisations to foresee and mitigate threats before they escalate. By examining extensive datasets, predictive analytics can identify patterns, detect anomalies, and anticipate future attack vectors, enabling security teams to act preemptively. This shift towards intelligence-driven security frameworks significantly enhances the resilience of organisations in an era characterised by increasingly complex cyber threats.

The Role of Data-Driven Security

Data has become the cornerstone of cybersecurity, providing critical insights into past attacks, emerging threats, and evolving cybercriminal tactics. Traditional security models often rely on historical data and static rule-based detection systems, which are insufficient against modern, dynamic cyber threats. Predictive analytics leverages vast amounts of structured and unstructured data from network logs, endpoint activities, cloud traffic, and third-party intelligence feeds to identify subtle indicators of compromise (IoCs). By continuously analysing this data, predictive analytics enables real-time threat detection and response, reducing the window of exposure to cyberattacks.

Furthermore, integrating predictive analytics with Security Information and Event Management (SIEM) systems and Extended Detection and Response (XDR) platforms enhances an organisation's ability to detect and neutralise advanced persistent threats (APTs). Organisations utilising predictive analytics can automate threat intelligence processing, prioritise high-risk incidents, and develop proactive security policies tailored to their unique risk landscape.

Artificial Intelligence and Machine Learning in Threat Detection

Artificial intelligence and machine learning redefine how security teams detect and respond to cyber threats. AI-driven security solutions analyse enormous volumes of data, recognise attack patterns, and dynamically adjust security controls. Machine learning models can be trained on vast datasets of malware signatures, phishing tactics, and intrusion attempts, allowing them to predict new attack methodologies before they are widely deployed.

Essential applications of artificial intelligence in cybersecurity include:

AI-Powered Endpoint Protection: Endpoint Detection and Response (EDR) solutions incorporate artificial intelligence (AI) and machine learning (ML) technologies to monitor endpoint activities continuously. These systems detect deviations from standard operational behaviour that may indicate a cyberattack. AI-driven EDR systems systematically analyse extensive datasets, including system logs, network traffic, and application behaviour, to identify patterns suggesting the presence of malware infections, unauthorised access, or lateral movement within a network. By using AI, these solutions can detect threats in real time and automate response actions. Such actions may involve isolating compromised endpoints, terminating malicious processes, and restoring systems to a secure state.

Furthermore, artificial intelligence enhances threat-hunting capabilities by correlating endpoint activities with global threat intelligence. Thus, it identifies zero-day threats before they exploit vulnerabilities. As cyber adversaries develop progressively sophisticated attack techniques, AI-powered Endpoint Detection and Response (EDR) solutions strengthen endpoint security against these evolving threats.

Behavioral Anomaly Detection: Machine learning algorithms continuously monitor user and system behaviours, identifying deviations from established behavioural baselines that may indicate potential security threats. These deviations include unusual access patterns, login attempts from unrecognised locations, and abnormal file transfers. Behavioural analytics relies on sophisticated User and Entity Behaviour Analytics (UEBA) models, which collect and analyse data from multiple sources, including endpoint activity, network traffic, and access logs. By employing AI-driven analytics, organisations can detect malicious insider activities and external threats that bypass traditional security measures. In contrast to static rule-based detection systems, behavioural anomaly detection evolves continuously, adapting to emerging cyberattack techniques to enhance detection capabilities. This proactive approach helps prevent data breaches, account takeovers, and malware infections by flagging suspicious activities before they escalate into significant security incidents. Furthermore, integrating behavioural anomaly detection with Security Information and Event Management (SIEM) platforms facilitates automated response mechanisms, reducing response times and enhancing overall cybersecurity resilience.

Automated Security Orchestration: Artificial Intelligence-driven Security Orchestration, Automation, and Response (SOAR) platforms significantly transform how security teams manage incident response. These platforms facilitate the automation of repetitive tasks, enhance threat analysis capabilities, and expedite the remediation of incidents. Conventional Security Operations Centers (SOCs) are frequently overwhelmed by extensive security alerts, resulting in alert fatigue and protracted response times. AI-empowered SOAR solutions effectively mitigate these challenges by automating threat correlation, risk prioritisation, and incident triage, allowing security analysts to concentrate on high-priority matters and threats. By integrating with Security Information and Event Management (SIEM) systems, SOAR platforms can ingest and analyse security alerts from multiple sources, applying machine learning models to correlate events, detect patterns, and recommend response actions. Automated playbooks streamline the execution of remediation workflows, allowing SOAR systems to autonomously contain threats, such as isolating compromised endpoints, disabling compromised accounts, or applying security patches.

An additional advantage of AI-powered Security Orchestration, Automation, and Response (SOAR) is its automated threat intelligence enrichment capability. This process involves collecting contextual information from various global threat intelligence feeds, monitoring the dark web, and analysing historical incident data to enhance decision-making. Consequently, this functionality empowers security teams to acquire real-time insights into the tactics, techniques, and procedures (TTPs) employed by attackers, reinforcing proactive defence mechanisms.

Moreover, AI-driven Security Orchestration, Automation, and Response (SOAR) platforms enhance collaborative incident response by integrating chatbots and virtual security assistants that deliver real-time guidance to analysts. These AI assistants analyse historical attack data, propose optimal response strategies, and dynamically modify security policies following evolving threat landscapes.

As cyber threats become more sophisticated and attack surfaces expand, the role of AI-powered Security Orchestration, Automation, and Response (SOAR) in contemporary cybersecurity operations is expected to continue growing. Organisations that utilise SOAR enhance their detection and response capabilities and optimise their security resources, improving their overall cyber resilience against emerging threats.

Deep Learning for Malware Detection: Deep learning has emerged as a transformative technology in malware detection, offering unprecedented accuracy in identifying known and unknown threats. Conventional malware detection methods, including signature-based and heuristic analysis, frequently encounter difficulties when faced with zero-day attacks and polymorphic malware. Deep learning models, particularly Convolutional Neural Networks (CNNs) and Recurrent Neural Networks (RNNs), have revolutionised malware detection by analysing extensive datasets and extracting features that effectively differentiate between malicious and benign software entities.

Deep learning-based malware detection systems function by analysing extensive collections of malware samples, thereby equipping themselves to recognise complex attack patterns that conventional methods may overlook. These models evaluate various inputs, including file structures, API call sequences, and network traffic behaviours, to uncover hidden patterns indicative of malicious activity. Furthermore, advanced deep learning architectures, such as Transformer Models and Graph Neural Networks (GNNs), enhance detection efficacy by clarifying relationships among diverse attributes within a malware sample.

Unlike static analysis methods, which assess code without executing it, deep learning-based dynamic analysis monitors malware behaviour in real time within a controlled environment, such as a sandbox. This approach enables security systems to identify evasive malware that alters its attributes to bypass traditional defences. Furthermore, deep learning enhances adversarial resilience, allowing models to adapt to new obfuscation techniques cybercriminals use. Deep learning models are integrated with Threat Intelligence Platforms (TIPs) to enhance accuracy significantly. Real-time malware threat data is consistently input into neural networks to improve detection capabilities. Moreover, machine learning approaches allow organisations to share anonymised threat intelligence across various industries while maintaining the integrity of data privacy, strengthening collective cybersecurity efforts.

However, despite its advantages, malware detection-based malware detection faces challenges such as high computational costs, dataset biases, and adversarial AI attacks where attackers manipulate input data to deceive detection models. To mitigate these issues, security teams must consistently update deep learning models with the most recent threat intelligence and utilise Explainable AI (XAI) techniques to interpret model decisions and validate their reliability in practical application scenarios.

As malicious software evolves, deep learning will play an increasingly critical role in cybersecurity, providing organisations with intelligent, adaptive, and scalable defences against the next generation of cyber threats. However, integrating AI into cybersecurity is not without challenges. Adversarial AI, where attackers manipulate AI systems to bypass security measures, remains a growing concern. Organisations must ensure that AI models are regularly retrained on up-to-date threat intelligence and monitored for biases or vulnerabilities.

Behavioral Analytics and Insider Threat Prevention

Among the most significant cybersecurity risks is the emergence of threats from within an organisation. Whether intentional or accidental, insider threats substantially challenge data security. Employees, contractors, and business partners often possess legitimate access to critical systems, complicating the distinction between everyday activities and malicious intent. Traditional security measures predominantly emphasise perimeter defences, leaving organisations vulnerable to attacks initiated by trusted users. Behavioural analytics is increasingly recognised as an effective solution for detecting and preventing insider threats through the continuous monitoring and analysis of user activity patterns.

Behavioural analytics employs User and Entity Behaviour Analytics (UEBA), which utilises machine learning and artificial intelligence to understand typical user behaviour and identify deviations that may indicate a security risk. Unlike rule-based detection systems that rely on predefined criteria, UEBA models dynamically adapt and evolve as they analyse increasing data, enhancing detection accuracy over time. By examining login habits, data access patterns, privilege escalations, and network activities, UEBA can identify anomalous behaviour that may suggest a compromised account or insider threat.

Key Indicators of Insider Threats

Behavioural analytics identifies signs of security threats, including deviations from normal behaviour and high-risk anomalies that indicate potential insider threats or compromised accounts. These signs are crucial for early detection and intervention, helping security teams distinguish between benign actions and those that could lead to data breaches, fraud, or operational issues. By using real-time monitoring and machine-learning-driven anomaly detection, organisations can create behavioural baselines that aid in identifying patterns suggesting malicious intent or unauthorised access.

The following are key indicators monitored by behavioural analytics to detect security threats:

Unusual Login Patterns: Employees who log into systems at irregular hours or from geographically distant locations that do not align with their usual working habits may indicate potentially compromised credentials or unauthorised remote access. Behavioural analytics tools track login trends over time, establishing baseline activities for each user. Deviations from these established patterns, such as unexpected access from multiple regions within a short period or frequent unsuccessful login attempts followed by a successful one, can trigger alerts that warrant further investigation. Furthermore, integrating geofencing techniques and risk-based authentication can enhance security by requiring additional verification when access attempts originate from suspicious locations. The combination of machine learning-driven anomaly detection and real-time identity validation enables organisations to distinguish between legitimate but unusual login behaviour and potential security breaches, thus facilitating a prompt response to unauthorised access attempts.

Data Exfiltration Attempts: Unauthorised data exfiltration is a critical indicator of an insider threat or a compromised account. This occurs when sensitive data is transferred outside the organisation without proper authorisation, often with malicious intent. Behavioural analytics plays a crucial role in identifying such anomalies by continuously monitoring data access patterns, file movements, and outbound data transfer transmissions.

Significant increases in file downloads, unauthorised access to restricted files during non-business hours, and using unauthorised storage devices, such as USB drives, may indicate a potential data breach. Furthermore, abnormal email attachments sent to personal accounts or unknown external recipients could signify a strategy implemented to exfiltrate sensitive information. Behavioural analytics tools utilise artificial intelligence to compare data access behaviours with historical trends, thereby identifying anomalies that may suggest a potential security threat.

Advanced techniques, such as Deep Packet Inspection (DPI) and Data Loss Prevention (DLP) solutions, enhance detection capabilities by thoroughly analysing the content and purpose of outgoing communications. Security teams are empowered to implement automated measures, such as prohibiting unauthorised file transfers, encrypting sensitive data, or notifying administrators when suspicious activities are detected. Furthermore, organisations must enforce stringent access controls and role-based permissions to minimise exposure to critical data, thus reducing the potential for insider threats and data breaches.

As cyber threats evolve in sophistication, malicious actors utilise encryption, steganography, and various obfuscation tactics to circumvent conventional security protocols. Organisations are encouraged to implement machine learning-based anomaly detection in conjunction with real-time forensic analysis to combat these threats effectively. This will ensure that potential data exfiltration attempts are promptly identified and addressed.

Privilege Escalation and Abuse: Unauthorized privilege escalation is one of the most dangerous cybersecurity threats. It enables attackers or malicious insiders to gain increased access to a system, resulting in data breaches, manipulation of system functions, or a total network takeover. Privilege escalation occurs in two primary forms: vertical escalation, wherein a user acquires privileges beyond those intended (e.g., a standard employee gaining administrator rights), and horizontal escalation, where an attacker laterally navigates to access accounts or resources for which they lack authorisation.

Behavioural analytics is vital in identifying privilege escalation attempts through monitoring access logs, authentication requests, and privilege modification activities. Key indicators of privilege abuse include repeated unsuccessful login attempts to privileged accounts, unauthorised changes to system settings, and unusual access requests to sensitive data repositories. Organisations are encouraged to integrate advanced Identity and Access Management (IAM) solutions with real-time behavioural anomaly detection to effectively highlight and respond to such activities promptly.

Organisations should enforce the Principle of Least Privilege (PoLP) to mitigate the risks associated with privilege escalation, ensuring that users possess only the minimum permissions necessary to perform their respective roles. Furthermore, implementing Privileged Access Management (PAM) solutions provides an additional layer of security by restricting access to high-risk administrative functions and requiring multi-factor authentication (MFA) for critical privilege modifications. Ongoing audits of user permissions, combined with AI-driven anomaly detection, enhance an organisation's ability to prevent and respond effectively to privilege escalation threats.

As cyber threats become more sophisticated, adversaries employ automated tools and exploit kits to identify and exploit privilege escalation vulnerabilities. Organisations must proactively conduct regular penetration testing and privilege access reviews to recognise security gaps before malicious actors can exploit them. By integrating privilege monitoring with Zero Trust Architecture (ZTA), organisations can significantly reduce the risk of unauthorised privilege escalation, ensuring that access is granted exclusively based on real-time authentication and risk assessment.

Sustained Lateral Movement: One of the most significant indicators of a sophisticated cyberattack is an adversary's ability to move laterally within a network. Lateral movement occurs when an attacker, having gained an initial foothold through compromised credentials or exploited vulnerabilities, begins accessing multiple systems or restricted files that exceed the standard scope of the compromised user's permissions. This strategy is often employed in Advanced Persistent Threats (APTs), where attackers remain undetected for extended periods, gradually amplifying their access and reconnaissance within an organisation infrastructure.

Behavioural analytics plays a vital role in detecting lateral movement by establishing baselines of normative user behaviour and highlighting anomalies that may indicate unauthorised access patterns. Key indicators include an account suddenly logging into unfamiliar servers, accessing data repositories it has not previously engaged with, or attempting to retrieve privileged information from administrative consoles. In many instances, adversaries employ Living-off-the-Land (LotL) techniques, utilising legitimate system tools such as PowerShell, Windows Management Instrumentation (WMI), or Remote Desktop Protocol (RDP) to avoid detection.

Organisations should implement a Zero Trust Architecture (ZTA) to mitigate the risk of lateral movement, thereby enforcing the principle of "never trust, always verify" for every access request. This approach involves network segmentation, which isolates sensitive assets from general infrastructure, consequently limiting an attacker's ability to move across systems. Furthermore, implementing multi-factor authentication (MFA), real-time threat intelligence correlation and deceptive security measures (such as honeypots or deceptive credentials) can aid in the early detection and disruption of lateral movement during an attack chain. With attackers continually evolving their techniques to evade detection, organisations must utilise AI-driven threat hunting and automated response mechanisms to analyse real-time behaviour, predict potential attack vectors, and respond proactively. By integrating behavioural analytics with Extended Detection and Response (XDR) solutions, security teams can identify lateral movement before attackers gain access to critical systems, effectively preventing breaches before they escalate into full-scale cyber incidents.

Proactive Insider Threat Detection Through Behavioral Analytics

To establish a robust defence against insider threats, organisations must seamlessly integrate behavioural analytics into their existing security frameworks, ensuring a proactive and dynamic approach to threat detection. This integration should not be regarded as a standalone initiative but as a fundamental component of a comprehensive cybersecurity strategy. By embedding behavioural analytics into enterprise security operations, organisations can enhance their ability to detect anomalies, mitigate risks, and respond to insider threats in real-time. The following measures outline the fundamental aspects of this integration:

- *Integration with Identity and Access Management (IAM) Systems:* Behavioral analytics can be integrated with Identity and Access Management (IAM) solutions to enforce rigorous access controls. For example, if an employee attempts to access restricted documents that they have not accessed previously, the IAM system can trigger additional authentication requirements or deny access entirely.
- *Automated Threat Intelligence Correlation:* Integrating behavioural analytics with real-time threat intelligence feeds substantially enhances an organisation's capacity to proactively detect and mitigate cyber threats. By persistently analysing patterns of user activity and juxtaposing them with well-established threat intelligence sources, organisations can ascertain whether a detected anomaly corresponds with recognised attack methodologies. This correlation empowers security teams to distinguish between innocuous deviations in behaviour and genuine security incidents, thereby diminishing false positives and concentrating resources on high-priority threats.

Advanced threat intelligence platforms aggregate data from various sources, including dark web monitoring, malware repositories, honeypot networks, and industry-specific threat feeds. AI-driven security tools analyse this data in real-time, mapping suspicious behaviour to known adversary tactics, techniques, and procedures (TTPs) as outlined in frameworks like MITRE ATT&CK. By leveraging this approach, organisations can anticipate potential cyberattacks before they fully materialise.

Moreover, automated correlation with threat intelligence enables predictive threat modelling, which helps organisations assess the likelihood of attack vectors based on current trends. This predictive capability allows for preemptive security controls, such as adjusting firewall rules, reinforcing endpoint security, and deploying deception technologies to mislead potential attackers. As cyber threats evolve, integrating AI-enhanced threat intelligence correlation will become essential for dynamic risk mitigation, enabling cybersecurity teams to stay ahead of adversaries in an increasingly complex threat landscape.

- *Real-Time Monitoring and Response:* Effective cybersecurity requires detecting and response to emerging threats. Organizations that utilize Security Information and Event Management (SIEM) solutions can incorporate behavioral analytics to monitor system activities, identify anomalies, and initiate automated response mechanisms. By analyzing extensive volumes of log data, network traffic, and user behaviors, SIEM solutions powered by AI-driven analytics can differentiate between standard operational fluctuations and authentic security threats.

To enhance real-time responses, organisations implement automated incident handling workflows that execute pre-configured actions upon detecting suspicious behaviour. These responses may include account lockdowns, privilege revocation, session termination, network segmentation, or dynamic authentication challenges to prevent potential breaches. Furthermore, extended detection and response (XDR) solutions improve real-time monitoring by integrating data from endpoints, cloud environments, and networks, thus facilitating cross-platform threat detection correlation. Organisations also employ threat intelligence feeds and machine learning models to refine detection capabilities, reducing false positives and allowing security teams to focus on high-risk alerts. Security Orchestration, Automation, and Response (SOAR) platforms also streamline incident investigation by automating data enrichment, correlating security alerts, and facilitating rapid decision-making. By combining real-time behavioural analytics, automated containment strategies, and AI-powered threat intelligence, organisations can significantly improve their ability to detect, investigate, and neutralise cyber threats before they escalate into full-scale incidents.

Adaptive Learning and Continuous Improvement: The dynamic nature of cyber threats requires an adaptive approach to cybersecurity, where machine learning models evolve in real-time to mitigate emerging risks. Traditional rule-based security systems demonstrate inherent limitations in identifying novel attacks, as they depend on static threat signatures that become outdated over time. In contrast, adaptive learning models utilise vast structured and unstructured security data repositories to refine their detection capabilities continuously, ensuring that defences remain robust against known and unknown attacks. By analysing historical attack patterns, network behaviours, and endpoint activities, machine learning-driven methods enhance their precision in distinguishing between normal variations in user behaviour and actual security threats. These models utilise unsupervised learning techniques to identify anomalies that diverge from established baselines, thereby facilitating the early detection of zero-day exploits, insider threats, and advanced persistent threats (APTs). Furthermore, reinforcement learning mechanisms empower these systems to adaptively modify their response strategies based on real-world attack outcomes, thus improving their capacity to neutralise complex cyber threats proactively.

Another crucial aspect of adaptive learning is its integration with Security Information and Event Management (SIEM) and Extended Detection and Response (XDR) platforms. These systems aggregate threat intelligence from various sources to comprehensively overview an organisation's security posture. As the cybersecurity ecosystem produces an ever-growing volume of data, machine learning models are more frequently utilised to enable distributed threat intelligence sharing without compromising data privacy. This decentralised approach strengthens global cybersecurity defences by allowing organisations to learn from attack trends across various industries and regions.

Furthermore, continuous improvement in machine learning-based security models is facilitated through explainable AI (XAI) techniques, which enhance transparency by providing human-readable insights into threat detection decisions. By integrating automated feedback loops, organisations can fine-tune their models based on real-world attack scenarios, reducing false positives and improving incident response efficiency.

Security teams must adopt an adaptive, data-driven approach to threat detection and mitigation as cyber adversaries refine their attack techniques. Dynamically evolving machine learning models, supported by threat intelligence and behavioural analytics, will be crucial for the next generation of cybersecurity solutions, enabling organisations to remain ahead in increasingly complex threat environments.

Challenges and Considerations

While behavioural analytics provides a proactive approach to detecting insider threats, there are challenges that organisations must address:

- *Balancing Security with Privacy:* Continuous monitoring of user behaviour raises privacy concerns, and organisations must ensure that security measures comply with regulations like GDPR (General Data Protection Regulation), CCPA (California Consumer Privacy Act) and other related acts.
- *Reducing False Positives:* Overly aggressive behavioural analytics systems may generate excessive false positives, leading to alert fatigue among security teams. Fine-tuning detection models are essential to improving accuracy.
- *Combating Insider Evasion Tactics:* Malicious insiders aware of behavioural analytics may attempt to mimic normal activity to avoid detection. Advanced AI models incorporating contextual analysis can help mitigate this risk.
- *Scalability and Integration:* Large organisations with thousands of users generate enormous behavioural data. Implementing scalable analytics solutions capable of real-time processing is crucial.

Future of Behavioral Analytics in Cybersecurity

The future of behavioural analytics is fundamentally tied to its progressive integration with AI-driven cybersecurity frameworks. Advances in deep learning and natural language processing (NLP) will further enhance behavioural analysis capabilities, enabling security systems to analyse user actions, intent, sentiments, and anomalies within communication patterns. Additionally, combining behavioural analytics with Zero Trust Architecture (ZTA) will reinforce the principle of "*never trust, always verify,*" ensuring that access to critical systems is continuously validated based on real-time risk assessments.

As insider threats continue to evolve in complexity, behavioural analytics will remain integral to contemporary cybersecurity strategies. Organisations that utilise AI-driven User and Entity Behaviour Analytics (UEBA) models will significantly enhance their ability to detect, investigate, and mitigate insider risks before they escalate into full-scale security incidents. Among the most significant cybersecurity threats originate from within an organisation. Regardless of whether these threats are intentional or accidental, they constitute a critical challenge to data security. Conventional security mechanisms focus on perimeter defences, leaving vulnerabilities in detecting threats from legitimate user accounts. Behavioural analytics effectively addresses this challenge by monitoring and analysing user activity patterns to identify deviations that may signify suspicious behaviour.

Behavioural analytics employs User and Entity Behaviour Analytics (UEBA), which continuously learns normal user activity and flags anomalies that may indicate credential misuse, unauthorised access, or malicious intent. Key indicators include:

- *Unusual Login Patterns:* Employees accessing systems outside of normal working hours or from unfamiliar locations.
- *Data Exfiltration Attempts:* Sudden spikes in file downloads, unauthorised data transfers, or access to restricted files.
- *Privilege Escalation Abuses:* Employees attempting to gain administrative privileges without authorisation.
- *Sustained Lateral Movement:* Indicators that an attacker, using compromised credentials, moves laterally within the network to escalate an attack.

By integrating behavioural analytics with Identity and Access Management (IAM) solutions, organisations can enforce strict access controls, detect compromised accounts in real-time, and prevent data breaches caused by insider threats.

Predictive Threat Intelligence and Cyber Risk Forecasting

Incorporating predictive analytics into threat intelligence enables security teams to forecast cyber risk trends and implement preemptive security measures. Organisations can anticipate future threats before they impact their networks by analysing data from threat intelligence feeds, dark web monitoring, and attack simulations. Cyber risk forecasting involves:

- *Threat Modeling:* Identifying high-risk attack vectors based on industry trends and historical incidents.
- *Dark Web Intelligence Gathering:* Monitoring cybercriminal forums, marketplaces, and ransomware affiliate networks for emerging threats.
- *Machine Learning-Driven Risk Scoring:* Assigning risk scores to vulnerabilities, systems, and user behaviours to prioritise security efforts.
- *Predictive Threat Hunting:* Utilising AI-driven models to proactively identify indicators of attack (IoAs) before their actualisation breaches.

Challenges and Considerations in Predictive Cybersecurity

While predictive analytics significantly enhances cybersecurity, it comes with its own set of challenges:

- *Data Privacy Concerns:* The vast amount of personal and corporate data required for effective predictive analytics raises privacy and compliance concerns. Organisations must implement privacy-preserving AI models and adhere to GDPR, CCPA and related regulations.

- *False Positives and Alert Fatigue:* Artificial intelligence (AI) and machine learning (ML) models may generate excessive false positives, resulting in analyst fatigue and inefficiencies within security operations. Continuous tuning and contextual threat analysis are essential.
- *Evasion Techniques by Cybercriminals:* Attackers increasingly use AI to evade detection, requiring security teams to refine and update their predictive models constantly.
- *Scalability and Cost:* Implementing advanced predictive cybersecurity solutions requires significant investment in infrastructure, skilled personnel, and continuous maintenance efforts.

The Future of Predictive Analytics in Cybersecurity

As cyber threats become more sophisticated, predictive analytics will continue to evolve, integrating autonomous security operations, AI-driven deception techniques, and Machine learning for threat intelligence sharing. Future developments will focus on:

- *Self-Learning AI Systems:* AI models that autonomously adapt to new cyber threats without manual intervention.
- *AI-Powered Digital Twins for Cyber Defense:* Simulating cyberattacks in virtual environments to predict vulnerabilities before they are exploited in real-world scenarios.
- *Decentralised Threat Intelligence Networks:* Utilizing blockchain and machine learning to securely share predictive threat intelligence across global organisations.
- *AI-Augmented Human Analysts:* Enhancing the capabilities of security analysts by integrating AI-driven insights with human decision-making.

By adopting predictive analytics, organisations can shift from a reactive to a proactive cybersecurity posture. This shift reduces response times, minimises the impact of attacks, and contributes to the establishment of resilient digital ecosystems. Given the continuous evolution of the cyber threat landscape, predictive cybersecurity strategies will be indispensable in safeguarding critical infrastructure, enterprise networks, and user data against next-generation cyber threats threats.

Emerging Technologies Shaping Cybersecurity

The integration of emerging technologies is fundamentally redefining the cybersecurity landscape, presenting both opportunities and significant challenges. While advancements such as quantum computing, artificial intelligence (AI), blockchain, and Zero Trust Architecture (ZTA) enhance security capabilities, they also introduce new vulnerabilities that cybercriminals attempt to exploit. Cybersecurity professionals must understand these technological innovations and their implications to build resilient security frameworks. This section examines the transformative role of emerging technologies in cybersecurity, highlighting their advantages, potential risks, and the strategies necessary for their implementation effectively.

Quantum Computing and Post-Quantum Cryptography

Quantum computing represents a significant technological breakthrough, providing unprecedented computational power capable of solving problems that are beyond the reach of classical computers. However, this very power poses a threat to existing cryptographic standards, such as RSA and ECC, which depend on mathematical complexity for security. The rise of quantum computing technology has the potential to render these encryption techniques obsolete, thereby endangering sensitive information and allowing unauthorised access by adversaries equipped with quantum systems capabilities. To counter this imminent threat, the cybersecurity community is actively developing post-quantum cryptography (PQC), a set of encryption algorithms engineered to withstand quantum attacks. Organisations must proactively assess their cryptographic infrastructure, identify vulnerabilities, and transition to quantum-resistant encryption methods. Standardisation efforts led by NIST's Post-Quantum Cryptography Project focus on evaluating and implementing quantum-safe algorithms to protect critical data. Embracing hybrid encryption models, which combine classical and quantum-safe cryptographic techniques, can serve as a transitional strategy to ensure continued data security as quantum computing progresses evolves.

Blockchain for Cybersecurity

Blockchain technology, known for its decentralised and tamper-proof ledger system, is gaining traction in cybersecurity applications. In contrast to traditional centralised security models, blockchain significantly enhances data integrity, identity management, and transaction security, making it as an invaluable tool for protecting sensitive digital information assets. One of the key benefits of blockchain in cybersecurity is its application in decentralised identity management. Traditional authentication systems rely on centralised databases, which are prime targets for cyberattacks. In contrast, blockchain-based identity verification systems allow individuals to store and verify their credentials securely, reducing the risks associated with centralised identity theft. Furthermore, blockchain-powered supply chain security ensures transparency and authenticity in digital transactions, effectively lowering risks related to counterfeit products and supply chain vulnerabilities fraud. Despite its security advantages, blockchain technology encounters challenges, including scalability, high energy consumption, and regulatory uncertainties. Unlocking its full potential will be essential as organisations seek to integrate blockchain into their cybersecurity strategies.

Zero Trust Architecture (ZTA): The Future of Network Security

The growing complexity of cyber threats has rendered traditional perimeter-based security models ineffective. Zero Trust Architecture (ZTA) is a security framework that eliminates implicit trust and mandates strict identity verification for every user and device attempting to access network resources. Unlike traditional security models that assume trust based on location or network perimeter, ZTA enforces the principle of "*never trust, always verify*".
Key components of ZTA include:

- *Least Privilege Access Control:* Ensuring that users are granted only the permissions necessary for their role, reducing the attack surface.
- *Micro-Segmentation:* Dividing networks into isolated segments to contain potential intrusions and prevent lateral movement by attackers.
- *Multi-Factor Authentication (MFA):* Strengthening identity verification through multiple authentication layers.
- *Continuous Monitoring and Adaptive Policies:* Utilizing AI-driven analytics to assess risk levels in real-time and adjust security controls dynamically.

The adoption of Zero Trust Architecture (ZTA) significantly enhances security against insider threats, ransomware, and credential-based attacks, making it a foundational cybersecurity strategy for modern enterprises. Organizations must integrate ZTA within their security infrastructures by leveraging identity and access management (IAM) solutions, artificial intelligence-driven authentication, and automated threat response mechanisms in order to establish a robust defense framework.

Cybersecurity in the Internet of Things (IoT)

The rapid proliferation of Internet of Things (IoT) devices has significantly expanded the attack surface and introduced new cybersecurity challenges. IoT devices, ranging from smart home systems to industrial control units, often lack strong security mechanisms, making them attractive targets for botnet attacks, data breaches, and unauthorised remote access.
Future IoT security strategies must focus on:

- *Device Authentication and Secure Onboarding:* Implementing robust identity verification and encryption mechanisms ensures that only trusted devices can connect to networks.
- *AI-Powered Anomaly Detection:* Utilizing machine learning to identify and mitigate suspicious device behaviour, reducing the risk of compromised IoT endpoints.
- *Automated Security Patching:* Enforcing secure and timely firmware updates to mitigate known vulnerabilities before they are exploited.

Regulatory initiatives, including the IoT Cybersecurity Improvement Act, promote the adoption of security-by-design principles, requiring manufacturers incorporate security measures into the development of Internet of Things (IoT) technologies from inception. As IoT ecosystems grow, organizations are obligated to implement comprehensive endpoint security solutions and to establish zero-trust frameworks to protect against emerging threats associated with IoT threats. As technological advancements continue, new innovations are significantly shaping the future of cybersecurity, presenting both opportunities and challenges. Emerging technologies, such as quantum computing, blockchain, artificial intelligence (AI), and Zero Trust Architecture (ZTA), are transforming how organisations secure their digital assets. While these technologies enhance security measures, they also introduce novel attack vectors that cybercriminals seek to exploit. Understanding the implications of these advancements is crucial for cybersecurity professionals who aim to build resilient security frameworks.

The Evolving Threat Landscape

As cyber threats become more complex, organisations must proactively anticipate and adapt to an increasingly dynamic threat landscape. Adversaries use artificial intelligence, automation, and organised cybercriminal networks to develop more sophisticated attack methodologies. These emerging trends highlight the primary challenges that cybersecurity professionals are expected to face in the coming years.

Rise of AI-Driven Cyber Threats

In the evolving cybersecurity landscape, artificial intelligence is a double-edged sword. On one hand, it has revolutionised the defences that organisations rely upon to protect their sensitive information. Yet, on the other hand, cybercriminals are harnessing this technology, enabling them to execute attacks that are not only more sophisticated but also exceedingly elusive. Consider the rise of AI-generated phishing campaigns, where the nuances of communication are crafted with uncanny precision to deceive unsuspecting targets. Then there are the insidious deepfake-driven frauds, which blur the line between reality and fabrication, manipulating perceptions with alarming ease. Furthermore, the automation of attack methodologies has streamlined the malicious endeavors of these cyber adversaries, allowing them to breach organisational barriers with astonishing speed and reduced effort.

Consequently, while AI protects our digital assets, it also equips adversaries with tools to undermine those defences. AI-driven cyber threats include:

- *Deepfake Social Engineering Attacks:* Manipulated audio and video content are being used to deceive individuals into divulging sensitive information.
- *AI-Powered Malware and Evasive Techniques:* Malicious programs use AI to adapt autonomously to detection mechanisms, making them harder to identify.
- *Automated Exploitation of Vulnerabilities:* AI algorithms can scan for and exploit system vulnerabilities at unprecedented speeds, reducing the time it takes to patch security gaps.

In order to mitigate the threats posed by artificial intelligence, organizations must invest in adversarial AI research, behavioral threat detection, and automated cyber threat intelligence sharing to stay ahead of emerging attack strategies.

Ransomware-as-a-Service (RaaS) and the Dark Web Economy

Ransomware attacks continue to escalate, as cybercriminals increasingly adopt Ransomware-as-a-Service (RaaS) models. These models empower individuals lacking technical expertise to carry out sophisticated ransomware campaigns. The availability of these services through dark web marketplaces has lowered the barriers to entry for cybercrime, resulting in a significant rise in ransomware incidents specifically targeting enterprises, government entities, and critical infrastructure.

To combat RaaS, organisations should:

- *Implement Robust Backup Strategies:* Maintain secure, offline backups to restore operations without paying ransom demands.
- *Enhance Endpoint Protection:* Deploy next-generation antivirus (NGAV) and AI-driven threat detection to mitigate ransomware infections.
- *Enforce Strong Email Security Controls:* Block phishing attempts that serve as primary entry points for ransomware payloads.

Cyberwarfare and Nation-State Attacks

Geopolitical tensions have increasingly extended into cyberspace, with nation-state actors engaging in cyber espionage, infrastructure sabotage, and election interference campaigns. These nation-state attacks often utilise advanced persistent threats (APTs), which operate undetected for prolonged periods, infiltrating governmental, military, and corporate systems.

Key strategies to counter cyberwarfare include:

- *Cyber Threat Intelligence Sharing:* Strengthening collaboration between governments and private sectors to exchange threat intelligence.
- *Critical Infrastructure Protection:* Enhancing security for energy grids, financial systems, and healthcare networks to prevent cyber-induced disruptions.
- *AI-Powered Threat Hunting:* Leveraging advanced analytics to detect and neutralise nation-state cyber threats before they escalate proactively.

Biometric and Identity Security Risks

Biometric authentication has achieved extensive adoption as a secure method for identity verification; however, malicious actors are increasingly exploiting vulnerabilities associated with facial recognition, fingerprint scanning, and voice authentication systems. Moreover, biometric spoofing, synthetic identity fraud, and deepfake-based impersonation attacks are emerging as significant threats to identity security.

To enhance biometric security, organisations must:

- *Combine Biometric Authentication with MFA:* Implement multi-layered authentication to prevent biometric spoofing.
- *Develop AI-Powered Fraud Detection Systems:* Use AI to detect synthetic identity fraud and prevent account takeovers.
- *Ensure Privacy-Preserving Biometrics:* Adopt decentralised, encrypted biometric storage to minimise data exposure risks.

Conclusion

The future of cybersecurity is being shaped by a continuously evolving digital ecosystem, wherein innovative technologies present both opportunities and unprecedented risks. As quantum computing, artificial intelligence, blockchain, and Zero Trust Architecture redefine the security landscape, it is imperative for organizations to adopt a proactive approach to cybersecurity in order to stay ahead of emerging threats. Integrating predictive analytics, AI-driven automation, and decentralized security frameworks is essential in ensuring resilience against progressively sophisticated cyberattacks. Understanding the evolving threat landscape is essential for governments, businesses, and individuals. Cyber adversaries are leveraging AI, automation, and deepfake technology to launch highly targeted attacks, making traditional security measures insufficient. To maintain robust security postures, organizations must adopt post-quantum cryptography, blockchain-enhanced identity management, artificial intelligence-driven threat intelligence, and a Zero-Trust security model principles.

Moreover, cybersecurity is no longer merely a technological challenge but a strategic priority that necessitates cross-sector collaboration, ongoing education, and adherence to global security frameworks. As threats grow more complex, the significance of cyber threat intelligence sharing, regulatory compliance, and ethical considerations in AI-driven cybersecurity will become increasingly pronounced significant. To maintain resilience when faced with these challenges, cybersecurity professionals must engage in continuous learning, promote innovation in security practices, and establish adaptive defence mechanisms that evolve alongside technological advancements. Through these efforts, businesses and governmental entities can build a future-proof cybersecurity framework that protects critical assets, safeguards user privacy, and cultivates trust in an increasingly digital landscape world.

9

Conclusion and Actionable Strategies

The field of cybersecurity continues to grow in complexity as digital transformation accelerates across every sector. Throughout this book, we have explored the evolving threat landscape, emerging technologies, practical strategies, and global frameworks shaping modern cybersecurity practices. This chapter concludes with key takeaways from each area discussed and provides actionable strategies that individuals and organisations can implement to build a robust and resilient cybersecurity posture.

In this chapter, we will discuss:

- Recap of cybersecurity trends and challenges
- Actionable strategies for building strong security frameworks
- Steps towards continuous improvement and resilience

Recap of Key Cybersecurity Trends

Over the past chapters, we have covered:

- **Advanced cyber threats:** Increasingly targeted and persistent attacks such as APTs, ransomware, and social engineering.
- **Emerging technologies:** Integration of cloud computing, blockchain, and quantum computing into cybersecurity practices.
- **Frameworks and governance:** The importance of adopting structured standards like NIST, ISO 27001, and GDPR for compliance and best practices.
- **Real-world lessons:** How previous breaches and incidents demonstrate the need for proactive risk management and layered defence.
- **Future directions:** Preparing for a dynamic threat landscape through predictive analytics, threat intelligence sharing, and resilient architectures.

Actionable Strategies for Organisations

1. Implement Defence-in-Depth:

2. Build multiple layers of security controls across endpoints, networks, applications, and data storage to minimise breach impact.
3. Regular Risk Assessments:
4. Conduct risk assessments at planned intervals to identify vulnerabilities, assess threats, and prioritise remediation.
5. Develop a Strong Security Culture:
6. Foster a culture of security awareness where employees understand their role in protecting organisational assets.
7. Enforce Identity and Access Management (IAM) Best Practices:
    - Adopt the principle of least privilege for all user accounts.
    - Use multi-factor authentication (MFA) across critical systems.
    - Implement **key-based authentication** and regularly rotate credentials.
8. Secure Cloud and Hybrid Environments:
    - Understand shared responsibility models with cloud providers.
    - Apply consistent security configurations, encryption, and monitoring.
9. Establish Incident Response Plans:
    - Develop, test, and refine incident response plans to ensure rapid containment and recovery.
    - Include communication plans for internal and external stakeholders.
10. Regular Updates and Patch Management:
11. Maintain systematic patching cycles for all operating systems, applications, and firmware to address known vulnerabilities.
12. Backup and Recovery Strategies:
    - Maintain offline and encrypted backups.
    - Regularly test recovery processes to validate restoration capabilities in the event of ransomware or system failure incidents.
13. Third-Party and Supply Chain Security:
14. Evaluate vendors and partners for security compliance, as breaches often exploit less secure third parties to target leading organisations.
15. Continuous Monitoring and Improvement:
    - Implement security monitoring tools and SIEM (Security Information and Event Management) systems.
    - Review logs, alerts, and threat intelligence feeds to adapt defenses proactively.

Steps Towards Building Resilience

- **Board-Level Involvement:** Ensure cybersecurity is a strategic priority with oversight and investment from executive leadership.
- **Cross-Functional Collaboration:** Integrate cybersecurity with business continuity, IT operations, compliance, and legal teams for cohesive risk management.
- **Adopt Zero Trust Principles:** Design security strategies that verify every user, device, and connection, regardless of network location.

- **Prepare for Regulatory Changes:** Stay updated with evolving data privacy and cybersecurity regulations to remain compliant and avoid penalties.
- **Invest in Talent Development:** Encourage continuous training, certifications, and skill upgrades for cybersecurity teams to stay current with evolving technologies and threats.

Conclusion

In this chapter, we learned:

- A **recap of cybersecurity trends**, technologies, and challenges covered in this book.
- **Actionable strategies** that organisations and individuals can adopt to build strong security defences.
- The importance of **continuous improvement, resilience, and proactive adaptation** to address the dynamic cyber threat landscape.

Continuous Journey

Cybersecurity is not a destination, but a continuous journey that requires vigilance, adaptation, and collaboration. As technology evolves, so will threats. Staying informed, building a strong security culture, and implementing layered, strategic controls are critical steps towards safeguarding the digital future.